FROM ANCIENT MACEDONIA TO MODERN-DAY INDIA—

where holy men walk across beds of burning hot coals without being injured . . .

FROM THE STEPPES OF SIBERIA TO THE ARIZONA DESERT—

where vast craters caused by some cataclysmic force mark the land . . .

FROM THE ENGLISH COUNTRYSIDE TO THE HIGH PLATEAUS OF CENTRAL AMERICA—

where gigantic drawings in the earth form intricate patterns and figures which can only be seen from the air . . .

Here is an around-the-globe tour of the many puzzling relics that have come down to us through time—from such concrete mysteries as the frozen mammoths to the questions posed by such past civilizations as those of the Incas and the Phoenicians to present-day sightings of the elusive Yeti and the Loch Ness Monster. This startling and thought-provoking book probes through misinformation, legend, and tradition to the very heart of—

THE WORLD'S GREAT UNSOLVED MYSTERIES

Big Bestsellers from SIGNET

The World's GREAT UNSOLVED MYSTERIES

Edited by

Martin Ebon

Ø

A SIGNET BOOK

NEW AMERICAN LIBRARY

TIMES MIRROR

PUBLISHED BY
THE NEW AMERICAN LIBRARY
OF CANADA LIMITED

NAL BOOKS ARE AVAILABLE AT QUANTITY DISCOUNTS
WHEN USED TO PROMOTE PRODUCTS OR SERVICES. FOR
INFORMATION PLEASE WRITE TO PREMIUM MARKETING
DIVISION, THE NEW AMERICAN LIBRARY, INC., 1633
BROADWAY, NEW YORK, NEW YORK 10019

FIRST PRINTING, MARCH, 1981

2 3 4 5 6 7 8 9

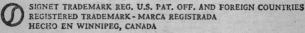

SIGNET TRADEMARK REG. U.S. PAT. OFF. AND FOREIGN COUNTRIES
REGISTERED TRADEMARK - MARCA REGISTRADA
HECHO EN WINNIPEG, CANADA

SIGNET, SIGNET CLASSICS, MENTOR, PLUME, MERIDIAN
and NAL BOOKS are published in Canada by The New American
Library of Canada, Limited, Scarborough, Ontario

PRINTED IN CANADA
COVER PRINTED IN U.S.A.

Acknowledgments

"They Walk on Fire, by Paul G. Brewster, originally appeared as "Ancient Art of Walking on Fire" in *Occult*, July 1973. Copyright © 1973 by Popular Publications. Reprinted by permission.

"Frozen Mammoths of Siberia," by Ivan Sanderson, originally appeared under the title "Ivan Sanderson's Study on Frozen Mammoths" in *Beyond Reality*, August 1973. Copyright © 1973 by Beyond Reality Magazine, Inc. Reprinted by permission.

"The Jinx Ship," by John Godwin, formed a chapter in his book *This Baffling World*. Copyright © 1968 by Hart Publishing Co., Inc. Reprinted by permission.

"The Mary Celeste Mystery—Solved?," by Dr. Oliver W. Cobb, originally appeared as "The 'Mystery' of the 'Mary Celeste'" in *Yachting*, February 1940. Copyright © 1940 by Yachting. Reprinted by permission.

"The Devil's Hoofprints," by Eric J. Dingwall, originally appeared as "Did The Devil Walk Again?" in *Tomorrow*, Spring 1957. Copyright © 1957 by Garrett Publications. Reprinted by permission.

"King Tut's Curse," by Gordon Thistlewaite, originally appeared as "The Riddle of the Pharaoh's Curse" in *Occult*, January 1976. Copyright © 1976 by CBS Publications, the Consumer Pub-

Contents

THE
WORLD'S
GREAT
UNSOLVED
MYSTERIES

Introduction:

Eternal Mysteries

Science and technology have shown us that they, and we, suffer from unending ignorance. No sooner has a technical or medical fact been established than new findings put it into question. The easy optimism of the nineteenth century has been replaced by the uneasiness of the twentieth. We keep discovering that yesterday's nourishment may be today's poison. All over the world, technology uses the bounty of nature carelessly, abuses the environment, ruins the very air, soil, and water of which we are a part.

And science has failed to answer a number of quite simple questions, some of them freshly put in this book. Despite our new machinery for analyzing archaeological remains, for judging historic events, and for tracing lost civilizations, much remains truly mysterious—things continue to baffle us, just as they did generations before us.

When our astronauts returned from the moon, we were told that the soil and rock samples they brought back would provide us with clues to the solar system, even to the creation of the universe itself. Things have grown rather quiet around these claims. We are now assured that it may be decades before all necessary scientific tests have been made. Meanwhile, our interest has shifted back from the moon to some of the mysteries that still remain on earth.

These are not mysteries in the religious sense, such as miraculous healings or divine interventions into daily events. No, we are simply concerned with such things as the vast destruction that occurred in the Siberian wilderness early in the century; we're still not sure whether a meteor or some other extraterrestrial event caused this huge destruction. We are concerned with such a relatively small item as a crystal skull found in Honduras, a single work of craftsmanship whose origin has never been explained.

And we are concerned with whatever fresh knowledge is available about the much-discussed Bermuda Triangle, about the Loch Ness Monster, about the Abominable Snowman, and even about the inexplicable ability of firewalkers to defy scorching heat by sheer faith. We have learned new facts about one of the weirdest mysteries of the Caribbean, the moving coffins of Barbados; perhaps our chapter on this subject provides a definitive answer to this long-standing question. In the case of the massive stone figures of Easter Island, we have painstakingly gone over the various hypotheses that are designed to explain away the mystery of it all—but have discovered that the mystery remains as impenetrable as ever.

We must admit, with all our twentieth-century technological knowledge, and even arrogance, that we are totally incapable of explaining something as old and as huge as the earth drawings in the Nazca region of Latin America. This is one of the most truly inexplicable artistic creations of all time. Yet, we don't even know who the people were who created these drawings, what they were designed to do, and why the tribes who made them disappeared without any other record of their existence.

Writings that can be deciphered by us are limited to the Near East and China. Other civilizations have come and gone of which we know only bits and pieces. The glorious palace of Knossos, on the Greek island of Crete, tells us much about the people who inhabited it, but we don't even know their name; we call them people of the Minoan civilization, although the King Minos after whom we named them was a mythical, legendary figure.

It provides us with a fresh perspective if, now and then, we stop to marvel at our society's ignorance. There is much we have achieved, much that scholars have painstakingly learned by methods of dating, through ingenious decoding techniques, or by electrochemical analysis. But much remains unknown, and we are far from knowing all there is to know—even with current methods—about our ancestors. The North American continent, Central Asia, and the eastern Caucasus promise archaeological findings that will vastly increase our knowledge. As recently as 1974, Chinese diggings in the city of Xai unearthed a whole army of man-sized figures, six thousand strong, carved centuries before the birth of Christ. Their ultimate meaning to the emperor who created them may never be known to us.

Of course, many more or less convincing explanations have been advanced, designed to tear away the curtains of mystery. Probably the most popular of all is the hypothesis that gods from outer space created many of the mysteries that continue to baffle us. And while this is an intriguing idea, which can be used to explain just about anything for which we have no final scientific explanation, it is really no more than a daring flight of fancy. Where there is no written record of a civilization, its remnants are like pieces in a puzzle that provide only a partial picture.

Still, scholars have made remarkable discoveries. Several of these are based on years of painstaking efforts to decode writings of the ancients. Perhaps the most striking example of scientific demystification was provided by the French Egyptologist Jean François Champollion (1790–1832), who used the so-called Rosetta Stone, found in a town at the mouth of the Nile, to establish a linguistic base for our understanding of hieroglyphics—and thus opened the gates to contemporary knowledge of ancient Egypt.

No such code has ever been found that might enable us to explain, for example, the Nazca drawings of Peru. However, we are indebted to an international group of scholars for the deciphering of the cuneiform tablets which have provided us with insight into the civilizations of the Near East, notably Babylonia. These stone inscriptions enable us to know the society, commerce, and beliefs of peoples who lived some five thousand years ago.

But where no such links exist, where archaeologists— and their new underwater colleagues, marine archaeologists—merely encounter yet another inexplicable remnant of an unknown civilization, the stones remain mute. Oral traditions last for only a few generations. Myths based on fact often become too distorted to suggest their original sources with accuracy. That is why it has been possible to use the Bible even for such precise purposes as the search for minerals in the Holy Land; no word of mouth, across millennia, could have retained the accuracy of the written word.

Yet there is an undeniable fascination with the silent evidence of past or lost civilizations. The colorful remnants of the Roman cities of Pompeii and Herculaneum, destroyed by the eruption of Mount Vesuvius in 79 A.D., speak to us without any contemporary account of this devastating volcanic outbreak. But even there, as in Knossos on Crete, all the vivid colors and well-preserved evidence of daily life fail to provide answers to many of the questions we still have about the cities' inhabitants, their lives and beliefs.

All of which should remind us that we know all too little—about the universe, our earth, even our own brains. There is little chance that we will ever run out of mysteries, in our own lifetimes and during generations to come. From infancy, we prove that we are born curious; and, happily, that curiosity will never be satisfied.

New York, N.Y.   Martin Ebon

They Walk on Fire
Paul G. Brewster

Firewalkers are practitioners of an ancient art that is more widely known today than in ancient times. When the firewalkers of the northern Greek town of Lankadas performed their ritual on May 21, 1980, onlookers included journalists and television crews from half a dozen countries. Nicholas Gage, reporting on the ceremonies in the New York Times *(June 1, 1980), quoted Dr. Christos Xenakis, who observed the ritual for the Max Planck Institute in West Germany, as saying, "If we could learn the secret of their incredible psychomastery over pain, it would be of enormous significance. I have examined the fire to see if it's hot enough to burn, and it is—250 to 3,000 degrees centigrade—and I have examined their feet to see if they are protected by thick calluses, and they are not." Mr. Brewster's article places the ancient art of walking on fire into global perspective.*

The fire in the long trench (twenty feet in length, two feet wide, and two feet deep) burns fiercely but with little smoke, as the wood has been drying for days. So intense is the heat that the spectators ranged along both sides and one end of the trench are forced to keep edging back from it, their hands shielding their faces from the glare. Here are gray-haired men and women, others of middle age, adolescents, toddlers, and babes in arms. Some are standing; others sit or recline on the soft grass. A short distance from the crowd are the members of the little orchestra. One holds a drum between his knees; another idly fingers the strings of a small lyre; the third holds a bagpipe. Although everyone seems relaxed, there is little or no talking and no laughter. One senses a feeling of eager expectancy. For the older people this is a familiar scene, to others this is a new experience, but in all, even the children, there is a quiet calmness.

Now the flames are beginning to die down, and soon the trench is a bed of red-hot embers. Men with long-handled rakes stand ready to make a smooth path of them as soon as the still-intense heat will permit a closer approach to the trench.

Suddenly all heads turn toward the open space at the opposite end of the trench. Walking in single file, a long line of men and women slowly approaches. All are clad in flowing white robes, and their feet are bare. The line halts momentarily at the end of the trench, and the orchestra begins to play a plaintive air. The leader of the line steps out on the bed of hot embers and, followed closely by the rest, walks slowly across it. Occasionally a walker stops halfway, shuffles his feet in the coals, and then proceeds. The only sound is the sharp drawing of breath on the part of the spectators. The walk completed, the participants go to a nearby stream to wash the ashes from their feet, after which they return to mingle with the crowd. There are no congratulations; there is no applause. This is a religious ceremony. This is the fire-walk.

Where was the setting of the performance just described? It could have been a temple or a shrine in Japan, a mountainside in Thrace or Macedonia, a Bulgarian valley, a courtyard in Spain, a lamasery in Tibet. But, wherever the setting, fire-walking is always essentially a religious rite. It is true that fire-walking has occasionally been performed purely as an exhibition, with no religious associations. Such was the 1930 performance in Baroda State, which has been described in detail by a British officer's wife who was one of the participants. But the fire-walking was part of the entertainment provided by the Gaekwar for his distinguished guests. The chief officiant was a Parsee who did no walking since to his sect fire is sacred. Although those taking part were barefoot, there were no burns; however, some of the walkers complained of severe pain at the conclusion of the walk. This the Parsee explained was the result of his not having prayed and fasted for a sufficient length of time.

Some years later, a similar demonstration was held at Rockefeller Center by the Hindu mystic Kuda Bux. According to official records, three cords of oak and five hundred pounds of charcoal burned for eight hours to make the bed of embers over which Bux walked unharmed. A pyrometer registered the temperature at 1,200 degrees F.

Fire-walking falls into two basic types. One of these is the walking over hot stones or other heated objects, a form prevalent in Polynesia. The other, much more widespread, is the walking over live coals, practiced in Greece, Bulgaria, Spain, China, Japan, India, Fiji, Ceylon, Thailand, Tibet, and the East Indies.

The manner of fire-walking varies widely. In the *Anastenaria*, as we shall see, the pace is leisurely and the walkers may at times stop for a moment in the middle of the walk. In Ceylon and Thailand the walkers almost run across the fire. Among the Kadar of India and generally in the Far East the walking is slow and deliberate.

It is believed by many fire-walkers that to be touched by an outsider during the walk is highly dangerous. The course usually followed by the one touched is the undergoing of a second purification before again attempting the walk.

Although fire-walking does not figure prominently among the North American Indians, it is occasionally practiced by members of certain secret societies among the Zuni and the Keresan.

However, of all phenomena, the ability of certain individuals or groups to walk barefoot through fire without being burned is one of the most spectacular and certainly one of the most puzzling. The origin of the practice is, like that of so many other strange powers, far from being definitely established. Most Eastern fire-walkers claim that it originated in Central Asia, reputedly the ancient birthplace of mankind, and it is well known that fire-walking has, from time immemorial, been a part of the stock in trade of the Asiatic shaman. In Europe it can be traced back to an ancient Roman family, the Hirpi, who, so the elder Pliny (A.D. 23–79) tells us, "at the yearly sacrifice to Apollo performed on Mount Soracte walk over a charred pile of logs without being scorched and who consequently enjoy exemption under a perpetual decree of the Senate from military service and all other burdens." This performance has been described also by the geographer Strabo (63 B.C.–A.D. 21), Virgil (70–19 B.C.), and other early writers.

MACEDONIA AND THRACE

This fire-walking ceremony dates from about the middle of the thirteenth century and has been performed annually without interruption from that time to the present. It is always held on May 21, the joint feast day of St. Constantine, first Christian emperor of Rome, and St. Helen, his mother.

According to tradition, the Church of St. Constantine in the tiny Thracian village of Kosti one day caught on fire. Since there was no firefighting equipment, the flames were soon out of control. As the villagers stood helplessly by, sadly watching their beloved church burn, suddenly there came the sound of cries from within it. When a hasty check of their number showed that no one was missing, the hearers realized that the cries issued not from human throats but from the sacred icons in the building. A few of the bravest dashed into the burning church, snatched up the eight icons, and carried them outside to safety without so much as a hair of their heads being singed. St. Constantine had performed a miracle! It was agreed by all that care of the icons should henceforth be entrusted to the heroes who had risked their lives to save them and to their descendants. The latter vowed that on each anniversary of the date, May 21, they would walk barefoot on fire, convinced that St. Constantine and St. Helen would protect them from injury. And they have kept their vow to this day.

Members of the brotherhood, the *Anastenarides*, live under very strict rules and must be obedient to the orders of their leader, who is regarded as their medium of communication with the saint. Each leader chooses his successor and trains him over a long period. No fire-walker participates actively unless he has been "called" by the saint (that is, unless psychic contact has been established). Those who are to play an active role are required to observe a period of fasting and continence before participating.

The ceremony begins in the *konaki*, the room in which the icons are kept. Here the fire-walkers gather to await the "call" of the saint. There is a period of brooding concentration in the sultry incense-filled room, and then the dancing begins to an air in two-four time played by the rude orchestra. After all who are to walk have received their "call," the group disperses until the following day.

In the meantime, long tables set up in the yard have been covered with candles, flowers, incense-burners, communion loaves, and a bowl of water (to be blessed later). Fuel for the fire is already in place, but it is not to be lighted until the leader gives the word, and he and the others wait in the *konaki*.

The sacrificial bull, with flowers fastened to his collar and lighted candles affixed to his horns, is led forward to be blessed by the officiating priest and to be sprinkled with holy water from a sprig of sweet basil. Before he is led away to be tied until the time of sacrifice, two of the fire-walkers perform a dance in front of him to put him in the proper mood. A few minutes later he is led in procession to the *konaki*, where he is tethered to a post. The leader of the fire-walkers makes the sign of the cross over him with the special ceremonial knife, then hands the knife to the butcher, who severs the bull's head from its body. The flesh is equally divided among the members of the brotherhood, and, according to custom, the hide is cut into strips of the proper size for making shoes. These are distributed among the needy.

9

And now the leader sends a messenger to announce that it is time for the fire to be lighted. In a few minutes the fire-walkers come out, the leader carrying an icon and his followers bearing icons or other religious objects, and march in procession to the fire, where a great crowd has gathered. Among the spectators are government officials, members of the diplomatic corps, *aolsiwea*, and photographers. Here too are physicians, psychologists, and psychiatrists, to whom the performance is of great scientific interest.

Arriving at the fire, the walkers rush out upon the hot embers and dance back and forth upon them, jump up and down, digging their feet in, and occasionally kneeling. Most are barefoot, but some keep on their rough woolen stockings.

After about thirty or forty minutes, the fire-walkers go back to the *konaki*, where they reverently replace the icons and then go out into the yard to rinse their feet. Immediately there is a rush of medical men eager to examine them. Tolerantly the fire-walkers present their feet, upon which no blisters or even unusual redness of skin are discernible even upon close examination with a magnifying glass. Aside from a slightly accelerated pulse and respiration rate, the participants appear none the worse for their experience. On the contrary they are completely relaxed and happy.

The lot of the *Anastenarides* has not always been a pleasant one. After centuries of peace and security in the almost inaccessible mountain district of northern Thrace, they were in 1914 transferred, under the terms of the Treaty of Bucharest, from Turkish to Bulgarian sovereignty. Disliking the change, they fled to the Greek motherland, where their ceremony soon became a target of the Greek Orthodox Church, which condemned it as pagan and idolatrous and forbade its performance. The walkers then "went underground," holding the ceremony in the *konaki* and without benefit of clergy. The ban was rescinded by the Bishop of Macedonia in 1948, but even today the fire-walkers are forced to find a retired priest of Thracian origin to officiate at the *Anastenaria*. There is also another and a more recent problem. Professor George

Megas, Director of the Folklore Archives, Academy of Athens, writes me that the great fear of the fire-walkers today is that, with the steadily growing public interest, what has always been a religious ceremony may degenerate into mere theatricalism. Older members of the brotherhood are beginning to look back with longing to "the good old days" and have even expressed a desire to return to their former privacy.

FIRE-WALK IN INDIA

Fire-walking is practiced in many parts of India, notably in the Madras area. It usually takes place shortly after the Holi festival (March) and is regarded as both a thanksgiving and a purification ceremony.

The first step is the digging of a trench about twenty feet long, which is then filled with dry branches and logs. After the offering of prayers to the deity, the wood is ignited and kept burning until the trench is a pathway of still-flaming embers.

Meanwhile those who are to walk have taken a ritual bath and are now at one end of the trench. Each carries a small brass or earthenware vessel (*khumba*) of water in which floats a bouquet of flowers and leaves intended as a shrine offering at the conclusion of the fire-walk.

The ceremony proper begins with the ringing of the temple bells. The fire-walkers step down into the trench, and in single file and complete silence they walk slowly across the red-hot embers, looking neither to right nor to left. During the walk, attendants constantly fan the fire with bunches of *neem* leaves, which are thought to be highly efficacious in warding off all evil influences.

Having arrived at the other end of the trench, the fire-walkers proceed to the shrine, where each empties the contents of the *khumba* before the statue of the deity as an act of piety and as penance for past wrongdoing.

An anthropologist friend, Professor U. R. Ehrenfels, who has been a longtime student of the Kadar of Cochin, informs us that among them the ceremony is performed before the temple of Muringayali in honor of Kundathi-Kali. During *Kumbalan* (in February) the devotees of Kundathi-Kali fast (as do also their families), take three baths a day, and refrain from chewing, from buying or borrowing, and from speaking to a woman. If all these injunctions have been scrupulously observed, the worshiper will be able to remove the bamboo posts held by two priests in front of a pit fifty feet long filled with burning logs, and can then walk unscathed across the fire, the heat of which will be miraculously transferred into two golden rods in front of the Kali image in the temple. After the successful termination of the walk, the devotee will have acquired occult power enabling him to remove evil spirits and fever from himself and others and also to inflict harm if he so desires.

FIJIAN FIRE-WALKING

Since a large percentage of the fire-walkers of Fiji are Hindus, it is readily understandable that the ceremony as performed in Fiji should resemble that performed by Indian fire-walkers. Many of the Hindu fire-walkers of the former claim that the practice was introduced into that country from Madras.

In Fiji the fire is personified as a goddess (her name varies with locale). Sometimes the term used for her is simply "the Power." The fire-walk is preceded by a ten-day period of purification during which those who are to participate may neither smoke nor drink and must abstain from sexual intercourse. During this time they live in an encampment near the temple, where they are under the constant supervision of a priest. Later preparation takes place within the temple itself. Here they perform a circle dance before the effigy of the goddess to the accompaniment of three drums (representing the Hindu trinity Brahma, Shiva, and Vishnu) and a conch. At times there is also a sacrifice of fowls or goats. In order to determine whether the intending walkers are sufficiently charged with "the Power," the priest lashes their bare prostrate bodies with a rope whip. If there is no blood or mark of the whip on the skin, they are adjudged fit.

On the morning of the day on which the fire-walking is to take place, the walkers go barefoot to a nearby stream, where they perform the final act of purification, total immersion in the water. Beside the stream is the *khalasam*, a brass pot about half full of water and having a coconut stuck in the neck. Transfixing the coconut is a wooden stick, one end of which rests on the bottom of the pot. The end pointing upward is in the form of a trident, the prongs of which represent the trinity. The entire top of the *khalasam* is decorated with *neem* and mango leaves, flowers, and fruits.

The fire-walkers now form a circle around the *khalasam*, and skewers and wires are run through their cheeks and the skin of backs, arms, and chests. There is no blood—final proof of their fitness to make the walk. The priest now sets the *khalasam* on his head and leads the procession back to the temple.

The red-hot coals having been carefully leveled in the trench, the priest, still bearing the *khalasam* on his head, walks leisurely over them, followed by the other fire-walkers. Some walk slowly like their leader; others pause and dance on the embers; a few dash across as quickly as possible. Burns result only if the walker has broken one of the prohibitions mentioned above or if he has been defiled by the touch of a nonparticipant.

SPANISH FIRE-WALKING

In Spain the practice of fire-walking appears to be confined, at least largely, to San Pedro Manrique. In fact the San Pedranos insist that only they in all Spain possess the requisite immunity to fire.

The ceremony is performed annually on St. John's Eve in honor of the saint. Apparently no purificatory rites precede the walking, and there are no prohibitions. The trench in which the walking is done usually measures only three by seven feet, a relatively small area. Accompanying music is furnished by the village band.

A unique feature connected with the Spanish fire-walk is the firm belief of the walkers that no one should venture out upon the fire without someone on his shoulders. This added weight, say the fire-walkers, is essential if one is to make the walk unburned.

13

TIBETAN FIRE-WALKING

Both the Lamaist and the Bonist priesthoods of Tibet regard fire-walking as an essential part of their rites. The walking is preceded by prayers and incantations. The priest then walks around the fire, three times clockwise and five times counterclockwise, muttering prayers all the while. Then he touches each participant on both shoulders with a feather-tipped wand and leads the group onto the fire. From this moment on, there is no sound except the high nasal chanting of the priest as they cross the white-hot mass of embers in single file.

For three days in March, beginning on the twenty-third day after the Chinese New Year, thousands of people gather at a shrine in Bangsue to pay honor to the memory of Chikong, revered by both Chinese and Thai.

Chikong was a patron of the poor and the underprivileged, often begging alms for them and always helping them in every way possible. He is said to have been fond of drinking and was never to be seen without his jug of wine. He always dressed in rags and wore a conical battered hat. On his back he carried a spiked mace, presumably for defense.

Although fire-walking is only one of the features (others are a ladder of sharp swords and a chair of nails), it is the highlight of the festival. The impersonating of Chikong is done by Somsak Thamwittayathan, who for seventeen years has served as a medium for him. He is believed to receive power from the saint while in trance and to be able to transmit it to others around him, thus enabling them to perform many extraordinary feats.

The medium, in trance, comes out of the temple, dressed like Chikong and carrying a jug of wine. He pours sacred water onto the hands of his followers, who then sprint across the fire in a group.

At the end of the walking, the medium blesses and anoints all the devotees who ask the aid of Chikong. Later, the food and gifts which have been brought to the shrine are sold at auction, and the proceeds are given to charity. (An account of one year's festival, some of which has

14

been quoted here, appeared in the *Bangkok Post* of March 12, 1972.)

JAPANESE FIRE-WALKING

In Japan, fire-walking is almost exclusively a Buddhist rite. In Yahomura (Saitama Prefecture) a fire-walking ceremony is performed at the winter solstice by Buddhist exorcists (*yamabushi*). It is preceded by several weeks of purification, at the end of which time hundreds of people from nearby villages and towns come to see the walk. The ceremony is believed to be highly effective in driving away evil influences of all kinds. In Miye Prefecture at mid-April the walking takes place in the shrine garden. The *yamabushi* erect a pile of wood, pass the sacred rope (*shime nawa*) around it, and then, to the accompaniment of prayers, set the pile on fire. After having purified the fire by throwing salt upon it, the *yamabushi* walk barefoot over the hot coals. A similar rite is performed at Fukuroi-machi (Shizuoka Prefecture). At the ceremony of Sanjakubo Akiba Sohonden (January 15), following the procession of the portable shrine, worshipers walk across hot embers at the bottom of a trench some twelve feet long.

Another ceremony in which fire plays a part, although there is no actual fire-walking, is held at the Ebiau shrine of Ishizumachi in Osaka. (This shrine is in a fishing community, and Ebiau is generally regarded by fishermen as their benefactor.) On the night of December 14, following a daytime ritual, devotees burn 108 candles of wood in front of the shrine. Around this big fire the naked young fishermen dance and jostle one another. After prayer by a priest, a young man, selected by lot and disguised as Ebiau, is taken up on the shoulders of the other fishermen and tossed into the fire, from which he escapes as best he can. They then extinguish the fire and march around the shrine three times, afterward carrying to their homes bits of charred wood as charms against evil spirits.

SINGHALESE FIRE-WALKING

The principal sites of Singhalese fire-walking are Udappu and Kataragama. In both places, the walkers fast on the day of the performance and purify themselves with a ritual bath just before participating. Dr. Kailasanatha Kurukkal, Lecturer in Sanskrit at the University of Ceylon, tells me that the ceremony is performed annually and always at night. There is no sacrifice and no music.

Logs, roughly the size of railroad ties, are built up in log-cabin fashion to a height of perhaps five feet, the inner space being filled with smaller pieces of wood and dry brush. The touch of a lighted match to the latter results in a roaring blaze in a matter of minutes. When the pile of wood has burned down to a bed of still-flaming embers, men armed with long poles level these and remove any stones or other foreign matter. The fire-walking does not begin until the fire is white-hot, with blue gaseous flames flickering an inch or two above the surface. As ashes form, they are removed by the use of large winnowing fans.

Walkers frequently carry bouquets of freshly picked flowers (which are unwilted at the termination of the walk!), and one of the photographs in my possession is that of an elderly man walking across the fire, carrying a small child in his arms.

VARIATIONS

Not all fire-walking is of the rigidly formalized type described in the preceding pages. On the contrary it is sometimes merely a *part* (and often a minor part) of a performance. The Balinese *sanghyang deling* furnishes a good example. This is a dance executed by two little girls in trance and supposedly under the control of two heavenly nymphs. Each stands on the shoulders of a man and there performs a classical dance in which she has never been trained, making the hand gestures faultlessly and swaying back and forth without once losing her equilibrium. Then the girls are taken to a temple, where a pile of coconut shells is burning in the center of the court. They dance in and out of the fire, scattering the glowing coals in all directions with their bare feet and sometimes even picking them up and pouring them over themselves. However, it is the dance at the beginning and not the subsequent playing with fire that is the *real* performance.

16

Another example of immunity to fire is sometimes witnessed at a Vodun ceremony in Haiti. When a worshiper "mounted" (that is, possessed) by Legba, Ogoun, or some other of the *loa* walks over fire at the will of his rider, this is only a small part of the whole Vodun ceremony.

EXPLANATIONS

Many theories, none of them wholly plausible, have been advanced to explain the phenomenon of fire-walking. It has been suggested, for example, that the speed at which performers cross the bed of hot coals prevents their being burned. However, as we have seen, walkers often remain standing for several minutes. Another suggestion made is that the immunity derives from the fact that the participants are accustomed to going barefoot and hence the soles of the feet are hard and tough. This explanation might be valid in some instances but would not hold good for the *alpargata*-wearing San Pedranos and the *tsarouchia*-wearing Thracians and Macedonians, the soles of whose feet are as tender as our own. To say that the feet are protected (at least partially) by a thin coating of fine ashes is hardly plausible, when, in Ceylon, the ashes are being fanned away during the whole of the ceremony. If the feet have been toughened by the application of certain ointments or herb juices, as has been conjectured by some students of the matter, how is one to explain the fact that stockings worn in the fire show no sign of scorching and that fresh flowers carried by fire-walkers are not wilted by a fire hot enough to make spectators move back several feet from their assigned seats? The suggestion that performers are in a state of ecstasy or a hypnotic trance which renders them impervious to pain would do nothing to answer the above questions, nor would it account for the absence of burns or blisters on the feet of the walkers.

Perhaps the best explanation yet offered, though this is not a completely satisfactory one, is that the immunity to heat is largely due to the way in which the fire-walker places his feet upon the hot coals, the principle involved being somewhat analogous to that operative in the snuffing

17

of a candle with the bare fingers. In other words, if the foot is placed firmly, the fire immediately under it is momentarily quenched, and before the fire at the sides of the foot can work in under it, that foot is no longer there. Thus, each step taken is in effect a temporary snuffing out of a small part of the bed of embers. However, this does not account for the fact that the flowers are not wilted and that stockings and other articles of clothing are unscorched. Fire-walking is *still* an unexplained phenomenon!

It Came from Outer Space

Michael Ballantine

What caused the giant explosion that hit the Tunguska River basin, in Soviet Siberia, more than half a century ago? Towns, villages, and whole forests were destroyed by a mysterious and powerful force, in the summer of 1908. Literally, the enormous force originated in outer space. The actual explosion took place some eighty miles above the earth's surface. But what was it? A cosmic body? A meteor? An unidentified flying object (UFO)? A comet? Or a spacecraft, on course or off course, that detonated a powerful explosive, or blew itself to pieces?

As the age of the earth goes, June 30, 1908, is just a few seconds ago. On that particular day, something happened that did not occur before, or since. If it had happened on just about any other place on earth, enormous damage would have been done, and every moment of the event would have been observed and narrated in dramatic detail. But because it took place in a remote region of central Siberia, the very nature and extent of this unprecedented event remained shrouded in mystery for some two decades.

On that day, early in the twentieth century, a gigantic explosion occurred in the region of the Stony Tunguska River basin, forty miles from the town of Vanavara. The

19

impact was so incredible that seismographs as far away as central Europe and the United States recorded the vibrations. The earthquake-recording apparatus in the south Siberian city of Irkutsk, more than five hundred miles away, registered severe shocks.

For many miles around, people were shaken and blinded by a tall pillar of fire. This conflagration from the sky turned whole forests to cinder, and burned the peat grounds for hundreds of miles from the center of the fire. One witness said that "the fire came by and destroyed the forest, the reindeer, and the storehouses." Afterward, when the Tungus tribesmen came to look for their herd, "they found only charred reindeer carcasses."

Using this eyewitness description as the title of their book, John Baxter and Thomas Atkins presented a narrative on the event in *The Fire Came By* (1976).

After examining the extensive documentation that has accumulated since the Siberian blast, the authors noted that "it remains today one of the greatest scientific riddles of all time." They added: "In Russia the event has acquired an almost legendary status. In addition to hundreds of scientific papers, the great blast has inspired countless stories, poems, films, and television programs. A bibliography compiled in 1969 by a Soviet periodical listed more than a thousand items published about the catastrophe of 1908."

However, back in 1908 the Tunguska explosion aroused virtually no attention in Russia itself. Central Siberia was remote. Political events in St. Petersburg (today's Leningrad), the nation's capital, absorbed public attention to the exclusion of odd and inexplicable rumors from faraway places. Yet, the impact of the explosion was such that skies in western Europe showed startling visual phenomena. The *Times*, London, published a letter from a reader who reported that she had found the sky on July 1 bright enough to "read large print indoors," while "the hands of the clock in my room were quite distinct" shortly after midnight.

Later, recalling the period just after the Siberian explosion, Spenser Russell reported in the *Royal Meteorological Quarterly Journal* (1930) that "a strong orange-yellow light became visible in the north and northeast," so that "twilight lasted to daybreak on July 1st, when the eastern sky was an intense green to yellow-gold hue." He added that "the entire northern sky on these two nights [June 30 and July 1], from the horizon to an altitude of 40°, was of a suffused red hue, varying from pink to an intense crimson." He noted that similar phenomena were observed elsewhere in Great Britain, as well as all over the European continent, from Denmark to Austria.

The New York *Times* correspondent in London reported under the heading "Like Dawn at Midnight" that, following a sunset of "exceptional beauty" and remarkable twilight effects, "the northern sky at midnight became light blue, as if the dawn were breaking, and the clouds were touched with pink in so marked a fashion that police headquarters were rung up by several people who believed that a big fire was raging in the north of London."

While Europe was awed and puzzled by these light phenomena, the Siberian frost settled down over the ravages of the celestial fire. On the one hand, the fire had melted large areas of the frozen peat and disturbed the growth pattern of the area; on the other hand, the severe cold quickly refroze the landscape in its new, distorted appearance, preserving the startling results of the explosion and fire which had ravaged the countryside, like a fly in amber. As Baxter and Atkins put it:

"In addition to causing a firestorm, the blast in the Tunguska region had radiated enough heat in a few seconds to melt the permafrost stratum to a great depth, causing swelling of large rivers and flooding. Before the early 1920s only a few of the bolder Tungus, at great risk to themselves it was later learned, had dared to enter this scarred region to see the damage. Indifference, misinformation, and falsely preconceived ideas, as well as the remoteness of the region, had helped to prevent any serious scientific investigation until then; but the official Soviet body, the Academy of Sciences, was soon to take the first steps that would begin to change this situation."

As is so often the case in the annals of science, the initiative for a continued investigation into the Tunguska explosion can be traced to one man—in this case, Dr.

Leonid A. Kulik, a researcher at the Mineralogical Museum in Petrograd. Kulik had come across fragmentary reports of the mysterious Siberian disaster. Apparently, he first read about the event in an old calendar which spoke of a "huge meteorite" that had been witnessed by train passengers near the town of Kansk. He also found a newspaper report, originally published in Irkutsk, which quoted peasants as having been frightened by a bluish-white light, a crash that resembled gunfire, and "a forked tongue of flame" which came out of the clouds.

Dr. Kulik had made a study of meteorites. The eyewitness accounts tended to substantiate the assumption that one giant meteorite or a group of small ones had indeed hit the Siberian tundra in 1908. Because reports on the explosion had come from a railroad junction at Filimonovo, Kulik's original writings on the explosion referred to the event as the "Filimonovo meteorite." He urged scientific and government authorities to enable him to visit the region in order to compile at least a preliminary report on the location and impact of the event.

The Academy of Sciences, which supported Kulik's successive visits to the Siberian region, arranged in 1921 for the researcher with his staff and equipment to travel in a special railway car on the Trans-Siberian Express. This train, which had been one of the great achievements of railway travel prior to the First World War, still suffered from equipment shortages and lack of trained personnel. When Dr. Kulik arrived at Kansk, he soon realized that the press reports he had seen were inaccurate. No sign of a meteorite was found. But he circulated a questionnaire in the area, which elicited a number of fresh eyewitness accounts and provided clues as to the actual location at which the disaster had occurred. As Baxter and Atkins put it, Kulik was looking for a meteorite, and "seeking the elusive proof of this became in time a life's work."

Another six years passed until Kulik was able to undertake a second expedition. The preliminary work was hampered by the reluctance of the Siberian people to speak of their experience; many of the Tungus regarded the gigantic fire and explosion as a supernatural event, perhaps divine punishment for their misdeeds, which might best be forgotten or at least ignored. Dr. Kulik eventually persuaded the Academy of Sciences to let him take enough staff and equipment to visit the region in the spring in 1927. Temperatures were barely tolerable, but the swampy tundra was at least passable.

All the traveling took a good deal longer than the planners had assumed. By June 1927, Kulik and Prof. Victor Sitin, of the Siberian Archaeological Society, were able to make an on-the-spot survey. Dr. Charles P. Olivier, chairman of the Meteor Commission of the International Astronomical Union, and astronomer at the Leander McCormick Observatory, University of Virginia, wrote in *Scientific American* (July 1928) that they "arrived with a very small scientific equipment, for they were unable to make many of the kinds of observations that Prof. Kulik desired, and which he states are necessary." Dr. Olivier, in an article titled "The Great Siberian Meteor," added that Kulik's findings were, nevertheless, "quite sufficient to prove that whatever did happen was the most astonishing phenomenon of its kind in scientific annals." The account continued:

"The central part of the affected area, which is altogether 15 or 20 miles in diameter, covers an area of several square miles and is situated on the plateau between the rivers Chunia and Podkamennaja [Stony] Tunguska, where there is a sort of enormous amphitheater formed by the surrounding mountains. This valley has many hills, swamps, creeks, and is largely covered by the tundra.

"The natives assured Professor Kulik that the whole valley was formerly covered by woods. The trees are now bare, without bark or limbs, and almost all lie on the ground, with their tops turned away from the center of the spot, thus giving a sort of fan effect which is plainly visible from the tops of some of the surrounding mountains. Here and there, some tree trunks still stand and, in a few isolated and very sheltered spots, some that are still living. But the region is in general now most desolate."

One peasant, S.B. Seminov, who was present in the village of Vanavara at the time of the explosion, told Kulik:

"About eight o'clock in the morning, I had been sitting on the porch with my face to the north, and at his moment in the northwest direction appeared a kind of fire which produced such a heat that I could not stand it. . . . And this overheated miracle, I guess, had the size of at least a mile. But the fire did not last long. I had only time to lift up my eyes and it disappeared. Then it became dark, and then followed an explosion which threw me down from the porch about six feet or more . . . but I heard a sound as if all houses would tremble and move away. Many windows were broken, a large strip of ground was torn away, and at the warehouse the iron bolt was broken."

Dr. Olivier commented that other eyewitness accounts spoke of burned storehouses and melted equipment, and confirmed the impact that ruined the countryside. He added:

"In looking over this account, one has to admit that many accounts of events in old chronicles that have been laughed at as fabrications are far less miraculous than this one, of which we have undoubted confirmation. Fortunately for humanity, this meteoric fall happened in a region where there were no inhabitants precisely in the affected area, but if such a thing could happen in Siberia, there is no known reason why the same could not happen in the United States."

The Kulik report prompted others to draw these conclusions even more dramatically. The *Literary Digest* (New York, March 16, 1929) wrote that if such a meteor had landed in New York, "it would have crumpled every skyscraper, and not one human being or animal would have survived." The magazine added: "And, of course, there is no inherent reason why a similar missile may not strike New York, Chicago, or any other spot, big or little, while the reader is perusing these lines." The *American Weekly*, Sunday newspaper supplement, reported the event in these terms:

"Scientists and novelists have tried to imagine what would happen if a comet or large meteorite struck the earth, but not until Professor Kulik came back did science have any accurate and true picture of what really would happen."

The paper referred to Kulik's second visit to Tunguska,

in 1928, this time reinforced by support from the Russian scientific community. The *American Weekly* stated:

"Last summer Professor Kulik made another search, accompanied by Professor Sitin and other scientific assistants. This second expedition, just returned to Moscow, brings the first eyewitness account of the scars left by this great cosmic encounter, also the first samples and photographs to prove earlier statements below the truth, rather than exaggerated.

"Over an area of three or four square miles, at the precise spot where the swarm of meteors hit, the ground is pitted and torn, Professor Kulik and Professor Sitin report, as though by long bombardment by the world's heaviest artillery. Pits and ridges and shell-holes alternate as in the most ravaged of European battlefields. Over the top of this utter devastation, the expedition found a thin layer of new moss or peat, as though nature were trying to hide the scar with the inconquerable vegetation of the tundra."

Everyone seemed convinced that a meteor or meteors or meteor fragments had hit the Tunguska area. However, even a six-year investigation by a team of Soviet mineralogists, published in 1980, failed to solve the mystery completely. Despite press reports of shell holes and a pitted surface, no actual craters were ever located that would have indicated a major meteor impact.

Meanwhile, expeditions to the Tunguska region became, in the late 1920s, more frequent and sophisticated. Not only startling still photographs were taken, but films of the expeditions and their findings were made by the Sovkino motion-picture company. Baxter and Atkins suggest that Kulik found himself in disagreement with Dr. E. L. Krinov, a mineralogist who lost a toe from frostbite during the third expedition, which began in February 1929 and lasted eighteen months. They say that Krinov felt Kulik should not have focused "his attention almost exclusively on what he was convinced lay hidden beneath the marshy turf of the Southern Swamp and instead broadened his scope to the larger region of the windfallen taiga."

Prof. Kulik, the two authors wrote, "obstinately persisted in his conviction" that there were crushed masses of "nickeliferous iron, individual pieces of which may have a weight of one or two hundred metric tons." Kulik estimated that the orginal meteorite, before hitting the earth's atmosphere, may have weighed as much as "several thousands of metric tons." Prof. Victor Sitin calculated that the metal content of the meteor, mainly iron and platinum, might have ranged, by 1929 price levels, from $100 million to $200 million in potential value. The *American Weekly* added, however, that it was "extremely doubtful" that "these metals could be worked profitably on a commercial scale in such an inaccessible and inhospitable region as that in which the meteorites lie." Baxter and Atkins summed up the findings:

"By the end of the 1930s the riddle of the great Siberian explosion was still far from solved. The cause of the blast itself was still uncertain, despite the work of astronomers, geologists, meteorologists, seismologists, and chemists and the resources of the Soviet Academy; and many aspects of the destruction site, such as Kulik's bare 'telegraph pole' forest around the Southern Swamp, remained inexplicable. Samples of soil from the fall point had been collected but not fully analyzed. Because Kulik had concentrated primarily on the central region and no expedition had yet explored the entire area of the uprooted trees, the precise borders of the destroyed taiga had not been carefully mapped out or examined. The exact shape of the explosion was not yet known, although Krinov had surmised from partial observations that it had an oval form."

The successive expeditions developed a campsite near the Southern Swamp, as well as a road from Vanavara to the point where the explosion had occurred. A small airfield enabled Kulik's last expedition (1938-1939) to take aerial photographs, which confirmed that the Southern Swamp had been the center of the explosion. The survey plane fell into the Stony Tunguska River, but Prof. Kulik and other passengers were unharmed. Three years later, after serving in the People's Militia in World War II, Kulik died in a German prison camp near Smolensk, on April 24, 1942. He was fifty-eight years old. His work was praised by the Soviet Academy of Sciences, which noted his "great persistence and enthusiasm," which had led to "concrete advance in our knowledge of the subject."

E. L. Krinov is quoted in the *Source Book in Astronomy, 1900–1950* (1960) that the investigation of the Southern Swamp and of the so-called "cauldron" as a whole did not provide "grounds for concluding that this cauldron is the place where the meteorite fell." He added: "But the absence, anywhere in the immediate or more distant neighborhood of the cauldron, of other areas that might attract attention as the possible places of the fall, the Evenki [Tungus] people's designation of the cauldron as the place, the coincidence of the cauldron's coordinates with those of the epicenter of the seismic wave, and finally the radial forest devastation around the cauldron—all point convincingly to it as the site of the explosion. There is only one possible explanation that removes the contradiction, i.e., that the meteorite did not explode on the surface of the ground, but in the air at a certain height above the cauldron."

In the decades that followed, the discussion about the causes of the Tunguska explosion ranged widely. A new generation of scientists, notably in the Soviet Union and the United States, presented imaginative, space-age hypotheses. The atom bombs which the U.S. exploded over Hiroshima and Nagasaki in Japan, at the end of the Pacific phase of World War II, created effects that could be interpreted as resembling the aftermath of the Siberian explosion. Did this mean that an atom bomb had exploded above the Siberian cauldron in 1908?

Even more challenging questions were being asked, provoked by the successful moon landings and other space feats by U.S. astronauts and Soviet cosmonauts. Had an extraterrestrial vehicle entered the earth's orbit, with either an accidental or hostile explosion resulting from this entry? Among the Soviet authorities who advanced such alternate explanations for the explosion was Prof. Felix Zigel, professor of aerodynamics at the Institute of Aviation, Moscow, who said: "Despite great progress in our knowledge of the structure of matter, we actually know little of the interior, 'submerged' qualities of such matter, or about the conditions which prevail as nuclear energy is released. Nor do we know for certain whether, on June 30, 1908, the earth may not have come into collision with a quite unusual, unknown but natural heavenly body."

With these alternative explanations in mind, Americans were interested to learn, early in 1980, that mineral specialists from the Ukraine had completed a six-year investigation of the soil in the Tunguska region. Theodore Shabad, writing in the New York *Times* (February 12, 1980), noted that with no "conventional" explanation of the explosion having won general acceptance, scientists in the Soviet Union and the West had begun to offer a variety of hypotheses, such as "an atomic blast of natural origin, the arrival of alien visitors in a nuclear spaceship, the fall of antimatter, and, most mystifyingly, an encounter between the planet and a black hole." He added:

"Getting down to earth from the flights of fancy, the Soviet press has now disclosed the discovery of tiny diamondlike grains, of the type that would be generated from carbon by extreme shock, as in the collision of celestial bodies. Such minute particles, together with greatly compressed forms of quartz, have been generally accepted as telltale indications of the impact of a meteorite fall."

The Soviet source for this information was the Moscow newspaper *Sotsialisticheskaya Industria* (January 24, 1980), which published an account of the six-year study undertaken in the Vanavara area by the Institute of Mineral Geochemistry and Physics, Kiev, attached to the Ukrainian Academy of Sciences. Under the direction of Prof. E. Sobotovich, head of the institute's Department of Nuclear Geochemistry and Space Chemistry, researchers had collected peat in the Tunguska area which was presumed to have been formed in 1908. Prof. Sobotovich told the Moscow periodical that the peat was then burned in experimental furnaces, and its ashes analyzed for their geochemical components. Shabad reported:

"From the start, the scientists identified carbon 14, a radioactive form of carbon that is made high in the atmosphere by the impact of cosmic rays and is used for dating geological and archaeological materials. The presence of carbon 14 was interpreted as evidence of the celestial origin of the material. Moreover, the percentage level of radioactive carbon in the peat ashes, the scientists said, enabled them to estimate the amount of celestial matter that fell to earth in June 1908. They calculated that it was at least 4,000 tons."

Prof. Sobotovich remarked that the researchers had not been specifically on the lookout for diamonds, but "when they took a closer look at the ashes, they noticed several minute black grains with dull luster and uneven surface." When viewed under a microscope, the grains resembled an opaque, dark type of diamond known as a carbonado. As no such diamond types are native to this Siberian area, Sobotovich concluded that "the diamonds entered the peat as a result of the fall of the Tunguska meteorite."

Did these finds provide a final answer to the Tunguska enigma? Dr. Sobotovich did not regard the geochemical analyses as the last word on the Siberian explosion, but expressed the hope that they would shed light on the mystery that has eluded a solution for decades.

Frozen Mammoths of Siberia

Ivan Sanderson

Mammoths of Siberia were literally deep-frozen during an unknown natural disaster. The freezing temperatures came so quickly, and were so penetrating, that they even froze the very buttercups that the mammoths had consumed and had not yet digested within their bodies. Ivan Sanderson (1911–1973), naturalist, world traveler, and connoisseur of the unusual, studied the mystery of the frozen mammoths for three decades. This intriguing contribution, written in Mr. Sanderson's characteristic conversational style, gained new importance in recent years: some Russian geneticists have considered the possibility of actually cloning a living mammoth from the cell of one of the frozen animals, a feat that is theoretically possible, although it faces many practical obstacles.

About one-seventh of the entire land surface of our earth, stretching a great swath round the Arctic Ocean, is permanently frozen. The surface of some of this territory is bare rock, but the greater part of it is covered with a layer, varying in thickness from a few feet to more than 1,000 feet, of stuff we call "muck." This is composed of an assortment of different substances, all bound together with frozen water, which becomes and acts like rock. While its actual composition varies considerably from place to place, it is usually composed of fine sand or coarse silt, but it also includes a high proportion of earth or loam, and often masses of bones or even whole animals in various stages of preservation or decomposition. There is so much of the latter on occasion that even strong men find it almost impossible to stand the stench when it is melting. This muck is spread all across northern Asia and is exceptionally widespread in Northern Siberia. It appears again in Alaska, and lies across the top of Canada almost to Hudson Bay.

The list of animals that have been thawed out of this mess would cover several pages. It includes the famous woolly mammoths and woolly rhinoceroses, horses like those still existing wild in Asia, giant oxen, and huge kinds of cats and dogs. In Alaska it also includes giant bison, wolves, and beavers, and an apparently quite ordinary lion as well as many other animals now extinct and some which are still in existence, like the musk-ox and the ground squirrel. The presence of the extinct species provides us with a fine set of riddles, and of those that are not extinct, with another set; and the absence of still others (like man) provides us with a third set. The greatest riddle, however, is when, why, and how did all these assorted creatures, and in such absolutely countless numbers, get killed, mashed up, and frozen into this horrific indecency?

There is one corpse in particular that is exceptionally irksome. This is the famous Beresovka mammoth that was thawed out of the frozen earth or "muck" of northern Siberia just after the turn of this century.

There was a time when there hardly seemed to be any real mystery here, apart from the preservation of animals long since extinct—in what was sometimes a perfect state. When western science first became aware of the matter, they summarily dismissed it with the classic statement that "the animals fell into the ice." And, for quite a time, this suggestion seems to have proved quite satisfactory to most people; those who murmured that one cannot fall into ice were hushed by dismal accounts of Swiss mountaineers falling into crevasses in glaciers.

31

It came to light, however, that there are not—and never were—any glaciers in Siberia except on the upper slopes of a few mountains, and that the animals are never found on mountains, but always on the level plains only a little above sea level. Further, it was pointed out that no bit of one has ever been found in ice. They are all in the muck.

These facts indicated water as the agency which engulfed the creatures. It was explained that they fell into rivers and were then deposited miles away in deltas and estuaries under layers of silt. This sounded splendid at first, but then the next group of riddles appeared. These animal remains were not in deltas, swamps, or estuaries, but were scattered all over the country. Almost without exception, they were stuck in the highest levels of the curious, flat, low plateaus that occur all over the tundra between the river valleys. It was also pointed out that the whole of Northern Asia, Alaska, and Western Canada could never have been one vast delta, nor could their rivers have wandered about all over this higher land, depositing muck *uphill*. But last, and worst of all, a number of these animals were perfectly fresh, whole, and undamaged, and still either standing or at least kneeling upright.

A mammoth falling into a river filled with meltwater is not going to be carried along in an upright position and deposited thus miles away. Also, elephants are very good swimmers in any case, and, owing to the huge amounts of vegetable matter they must keep in their stomachs at all times and which develop much gas, it is well-nigh impossible to sink them. Before this can be accomplished they have to be in an advanced state of decomposition or even to have burst. Then their remains would be shoved, bumped and probably rolled over and over along the bottom of the river before coming to rest in their final silty graves. But these standing animals were perfect, not burst, and with their fur coats in good order; they were not decomposed. On the contrary, their flesh was perfectly preserved. So the water theory had to be abandoned.

Next, mud became popular. There are certain kinds of clays found on the tundra only a few inches of which are sticky enough to hold a man by his feet; and so some intrepid Russian scientists suggested that, given a few feet of this substance, it could hold a mammoth till he froze to death. Despite the fact that no such substance has ever been found either holding or lying under any frozen animal, this idea at first came almost as a relief and was heartily adopted by almost everybody. But there are always, it seems, some spoil-sports in mammoth hunting; they pointed out not only the above fact but also that this hypothetical "goo" would have had to be unfrozen at the time, and that this could only mean that the temperature of the air was well above freezing. The animals must therefore have been frozen *after* death—probably by starvation—in which case they would have fallen over and started to decompose. Two emendations were therefore proposed.

The first was the idea that the animals fell into gulches, breaking down the banks as they fell and being engulfed in mud, and then that a sudden drop in temperature took place and they were frozen, upright. The other was that, after they got stuck, a gigantic blizzard blew up and froze both them and the goo forever. Both theories sounded possible, but both were immediately shown to be impossible. It was particularly this Beresovka specimen that proved this.

The Beresovka mammoth was discovered by a Siberian tribesman around the turn of the century. It was sticking head first out of a bank of the Beresovka River, a tributary of the mighty Kolyma which empties into the Arctic Ocean. This man axed off the tusks and took them to sell at the nearest trading post, at Yakutsk, and there he told the Cossack who bought them about the rest of the animal. Now there was an ukase promulgated by the czar in force at that time, stating that all mammoth or other frozen-animal discoveries were to be reported to the government. This the Cossack did, and a scientific expedition was sent by the National Academy of Sciences from St. Petersburg. The members of this company built a shack over the corpse and lighted fires within to thaw it out. They then dismembered it carefully, packed up the parts, refroze them in the air outside, and sledded them to the Trans-Siberian Railroad.

This corpse was sort of squatting at the back end, but

was raised on one foreleg in front, with the other held forward as if about to salute. Much of the head, which was sticking out of the bank, had been eaten down to the bone by local wolves and other animals, but of the rest most was perfect. Most important, however, was that the lips, the lining of the mouth, and the tongue were preserved. Upon the last, as well as between the teeth, were portions of the animal's last meal, which for some almost incomprehensible reason it had not had time to swallow.

This meal proved to have been composed of delicate sedges and grasses and—most amazing of all—fresh buttercup flowers. The stomach contained many more quarts of similar material. This discovery, in one fell swoop, just about demolished all the previous theories about the origin of these frozen animals and negated almost everything that was subsequently put forward. In fact, it presented a royal flush of new riddles.

First, the mammoth was upright, but it had a broken hip. Second, its exterior was whole and perfect, with none of its two-foot-long shaggy fur rubbed or torn off. Third, it was fresh; its parts, although they started to rot when the heat of the fire got at them, were just as they had been in life; the stomach contents had not begun to decompose. Finally, there were these buttercups on its tongue.

Perhaps none of these things sound very startling at first, but if you will examine them, one at a time, employing simple logic and good, common horse-sense, you will immediately find that they add up to an incredible picture. Let us take the points in succession.

That the animal had a broken hip shows that some very strong force must have been exerted upon it either before or after death. By the position of the corpse it would at first seem that this was caused before death by the animal's falling into one of the famous gulches and then having struggled to get out with its forefeet. However, there is no reason why the fracture could not have taken place after the animal was dead and be due to some great weight placed upon it while loose material remained beneath it. The animal may, indeed, have slipped and injured itself, though from what or into what there is absolutely no evidence. It had obviously not been either inundated or washed away by a flood, and it had not been drowned. Third, and very importantly, it was not only frozen but perfectly so.

The flesh of many of the animals found in the muck must have been very rapidly and deeply frozen, for its cells were not burst and, although one mammoth has been found by the radiocarbon dating method to be just over 10,000 years old, the flesh of these animals was remarkably fresh and some was devoured by the explorers' sled dogs.

At minus 40 degrees Fahrenheit, it takes twenty minutes to quick-freeze a dead turkey and thirty to preserve a whole side of beef. But these are mere bits of meat, not live animals clothed in fur and containing blood, internal organs, and food, at a living temperature of about 98 degrees.

The problem is to extract all the heat from the whole beast, but this can only be done from the outside—and by working inward. Unless we have tremendous cold outside, the center of the animal—and notably its stomach—will remain comparatively warm for some time, probably long enough for decomposition to start in its contents, while the actual chilling of the flesh will be slow enough for large crystals to form within its cells. Neither event occurred with the mammoths.

Here we must digress for a moment to consider a related riddle—namely, how these animals were all killed so suddenly. (And please note, I do not mean at the same time). Temperatures of lower than minus 100 degrees Fahrenheit have recently been recorded in Antarctica, and the air customarily registers much less than zero over wide areas of the earth, yet very large numbers of animals live happily at such temperatures. Sled dogs burrow into the snow to sleep in Antarctica and thereby obtain some protection, but they also stand about in the open for hours, even when a near hurricane is blowing—and moving air has a much greater chilling effect than still air. Men, though admittedly well clothed, have been out in temperatures of minus 100 degrees for up to half an hour—and in a roaring blizzard to boot—without their lungs freezing; but much more amazing were the little Shetland ponies that Scott took on his ill-fated dash to the South Pole in 1911. He got these to the dome of the Antarctic icecap, and they had to stand out in the open all the time, yet they survived as long as their food supply lasted. In fact, it takes a very great deal of cold to kill a warm-blooded animal, and especially one that is already somewhat inured to it.

It now transpires, from several studies, that mammoths, though covered in a thick underwool and a long overcoat—and in some cases having quite a layer of fat—were not specially designed for arctic conditions; a little further consideration will make it plain that they did not live in such conditions.

That they did not live perpetually or even all year round on the arctic tundra is really very obvious. First, the average Indian elephant, which is a close relative of the mammoth and just about the same size, has to have several hundred pounds of food daily just to survive. For more than six months of the year, there is nothing for any such creature to eat on the tundra, and yet there were tens of thousands of mammoths. Further, not one trace of pine needles or of the leaves of any other trees were in the stomach of the Beresovka mammoth; little flowering buttercups, tender sedges, and grasses were found exclusively. Buttercups will not grow even at 40 degrees, and they cannot flower in the absence of sunlight. A detailed analysis of the contents of the Beresovka mammoth's stomach brought to light a long list of plants, some of which still grow in the arctic, but are actually much more typical of *southern* Siberia today. Therefore, the mammoths either made annual migrations north for the short summer, or the part of the earth where their corpses are found today was somewhere else in warmer latitudes at the time of their death, or both.

Here is a really shocking (to our previous way of thinking) picture: Vast herds of enormous, well-fed beasts not specifically designed for extreme cold, placidly feeding in sunny pastures, delicately plucking flowering buttercups, at a temperature in which we would probably not even have needed an overcoat. Suddenly they were killed and sometimes without any visible sign of violence and before they could so much as swallow a last mouthful of food, and then were quick-frozen so rapidly that every cell of their bodies is perfectly preserved, despite their great bulk and their high temperature. What, we may well ask, could possibly do this?

Fossils of plants requiring sunlight every day of the year—which is far from the condition pertaining about the poles—have been found in Greenland and on Antarctica. This alone proves that at some time in the past either the poles have not been where they are now, or those portions of the earth's surface that lie about the poles today were once elsewhere. Astronomers and engineers concur in stating that the rotational axis of the earth cannot ever have shifted because the earth is a vast flywheel, and even if any force great enough could be found to so shift it, it would fly apart.

Ergo, the crust of the earth must have shifted. Whether it did so in bits and the bits then shifted around reciprocally as suggested by Wegener, or whether it moved as a whole as propounded by Hapgood, cannot be debated here. The latter seems the more probable at present, but in either case, if the crust does from time to time come unstuck from the central body of the spinning earth, it will start to move and new parts of it will drift in under the poles. However, the circumference at the equator bulges by twenty-six miles compared with the mean average circumference of the earth as measured north and south through the poles. This means that any portion of the crust heading for the equator is going to have to stretch by thirteen miles, while any moving toward a pole will have to contract by the same amount. And what must then happen?

The crust of the earth is estimated to be variously between twenty and sixty miles thick. This is really very little compared to the whole earth, being only about as thick as the outer skin of an onion. Its rocks are to some extent plastic, but are like taffy in that they can be stretched slowly, but will break if pulled too fast. Therefore, if a part of the crust goes up over the rise of the equator too fast, it will crack open and form vast rock-bergs, while the material from the layer beneath it will come welling up to fill these cracks and sometimes even to flow out in great sheets such as are found all over the earth. Also, both about the equator and toward the poles, where the crust is being squeezed, every available volcano will be set off.

Now, volcanoes, when in eruption, not only spew out lava and hurl out rocks but also eject masses of dust particles, steam, and other gases. Some of the dust may be shot into the upper atmosphere and then drift all around the earth. After the Indonesian island of Krakatoa blew up in 1883, there were magnificent sunsets all over the earth for several years because of this dust. Other great volcanic eruptions have actually affected rainfall, because moisture gathers around small particles, and the gases—notably carbon dioxide, if present—have a marked effect upon the content of the atmosphere. It has been estimated that if only twenty major volcanoes went off at the same time, all manner of positively terrifying things could happen to our old earth and thus also to both us and mammoths. In fact, this may be the answer to most of our riddles. This theory is buttressed by the fact that great layers of volcanic dust have been found interlarded with the muck in Alaska.

A sudden mass extrusion of dust and gases would cause the formation of monstrous amounts of rain and snow, and it might even be so heavy as to cut out sunlight altogether for days, weeks, or months if the crustal movements continued. Winds beyond anything known today would be whipped up, and cold fronts of vast lengths would build up, with violent extremes of temperature on either side. There would be forty days and nights of snow in one place, continent-wide floods in another, and roaring hurricanes, seaquakes, and earthquakes bringing on landslides and tsunamis (so-called tidal waves) in others, and many other disturbances. But perhaps most important may have been the gases, which would probably have been shot up highest of all. What would happen to them?

And this is where we get back to quick-freezing mammoths, for frozen-food experts have pointed out that to do this, starting with a healthy, live specimen, you would have to drop the temperature of the air surrounding it down to a point well below minus 150 degrees Fahrenheit. There are two ways of freezing rapidly—one is by the blast method, the other by the mist process; these terms explain themselves. Moreover, the colder air or any other gas becomes, the heavier it gets. If these volcanic gases went up far enough they would be violently chilled and then, as they spiraled toward the poles, as all the atmosphere in time does, they would begin to descend. When they came upon a warm layer of air, they would weigh down upon it and pull all the heat out of it and then would eventually fall through it, probably with increasing momentum and perhaps in great blobs, pouring down through the weakest spot. And if they did this, the blob would displace the air already there, outward in all directions and with the utmost violence. Such descending gases might well be cold enough to kill and then instantly freeze a mammoth.

Consider now our poor mammoth placidly munching away in his meadow, perhaps even under a warm sun. The sky need not even cloud over, and there need not even be a dust haze where he is living, which would appear to have then been about where Central Asia is today. All of a sudden, in a matter of minutes, the air begins to move in that peculiar way one may experience at the end of the arctic summer when the first cold front descends and the temperature may drop 60 degrees in an hour.

All the mammoth feels is a sudden violent tingling all over his skin and a searing pain in his lungs; the air seems suddenly to have turned to fire. He takes a few breaths and expires, his lungs, throat, eyeballs, ears, and outer skin already crystallized. If he is near the center of the blob, the terrible cold envelops him, and in a few hours he is a standing monument of what is virtually "rock." Nor need there be any violence until the snow comes softly to pile up on him and bury him. And here we leave him for a moment and turn to his distant cousin chewing away in Alaska, just outside the area where the blob descends. What happens to him?

The sky here probably does cloud over, and it may even start to snow, something he has not before encountered in September, when he is in the north on his summer migration. He starts to pad off for cover. But then comes a wind that rapidly grows and grows in fury and explodes into something unimaginable. He is lifted off his feet and, along with bison, lion, beaver from ponds, and fish from rivers, is hurled against trees and rocks, torn literally to bits, and then bowled along to be finally flung into a seething caldron of water, mud, shattered trees, boulders, mangled grass and shrubbery, and bits of his fellows and other animals. Then comes the cold that freezes the whole lot, and finally when the holocaust is over, the snow to cover it all.

This is exactly the state of affairs that we find in Alaska, where the mammoths and other animals, with one or two significant exceptions, were all literally torn to pieces while still fresh. Young and old alike were cast about, mangled, and then frozen. There are also, however, other areas where the animals are mangled, but had time to decompose before being frozen; and still others where they decomposed down to bones and were then either frozen or not. Beyond these again, there are similar vast masses of animals, including whole herds or families, all piled together into gullies and riverbeds and other holes, where only bones remain.

Here may be the answer to our riddle of why we find mammoths with buttercups in their teeth in one place, shredded but still-edible mammoths in another, rotting mammoths in a third, and mammoth boneyards somewhere else. The animals were frozen whole where the blobs of cold air descended before the winds began, shredded and frozen where the winds came before the cold had spread out, and reduced to bones where the animals had time to decompose before the cold reached them or where it failed to reach.

The remains, if still sticking out of the ground where the middle of the blob occurred, would have been safely sealed in if snow came, as the Beresovka mammoth probably was. A true icecap never formed in Siberia, but there is evidence that one once started to grow there; it soon died away, and as it did so, vast floods of meltwater brought great quantities of silt *down* from the south— which is the direction the rivers flow in Siberia—and deposited it upon the compacted snow. This froze in the fall, but melted in the spring, and since a dark material absorbs more heat, it gradually, year by year, dissolved the snow below and descended upon and eventually enveloped the quick-frozen mammoth by the slow substitution of chilled silt for compacted snow.

This does not, of course, purport to be *the* explanation of this singular phenomenon, nor is it put forward as more than just one possible way in which what is observed could have come about. There are aspects of it that don't quite jell—and perhaps this is for once an excusable pun. Principal among these is the extremely knotty question (an inexcusable one) of just how a frozen mammoth or anything else above ground actually got into a stratum of frozen muck which is rock-hard. This is the conundrum that annoys everybody and the one over which the "experts" invariably stumble. And stumble they have, ending with a veritable outburst by a leading buffoon in a frightfully august scientific publication a few years ago (whose name shall remain off the record as I do not wish to subject anybody to outright ridicule). Trouble is, nobody has yet thought up even a possible explanation for this business apart from the one quoted above, and this, as I say, is more than just dubious. Let us examine the matter, disregarding the *causes* of whatever did happen.

In order to freeze, or rather deep-freeze, a large elephantine you have not only to *freeze* it (externally) but literally *deep*-freeze it right to its middle, and bloody fast to boot; otherwise, first the contents of its alimentary tract, and then all its internal organs, will start literally to "cook" due to the release of heat from bacterial action as in a vegetable compost heap. Now, there are those who state that this is just the way in which the insides of these mammoths *did* get themselves preserved, and I will second the motion in that I once spent three weeks on a tropical beach cutting up a fifty-foot sperm whale that had manifestly been dead for months, and found that the muscular tissue deep inside was perfectly "fresh" and neither "blue" (as we say of completely raw steaks) nor overdone. So far so good, at least for the inside; but what of the outside?

If there was a drop of some 150 to 200 degrees in the air temperature, the integument and any bits and pieces sticking out, like eyeballs and genitalia, would

41

indeed be almost instantly deep-frozen. However, the (non-deep-freeze) expert should be informed that such an outer coating of deep-freeze is the best way to insulate the next layers within a solid, sealed body. Don't forget that "cold" is not the opposite of "heat"; it is the natural state, while heat is but a molecular agitation. Thus, you cannot draw cold out of anything, but you can dissipate heat. By this score, "cold" cannot diffuse into a body; rather, said body has to disseminate or diffuse its heat, thereby becoming what we call "colder"; and in the case of a thing like a mammoth this will take quite some time when it is enshrined in an insulating capsule of deep-freeze. So there are problems in the middle layers too.

But next, the really vital question. Whether you get the damned thing deep-frozen all through or not, how do you get it into a solid mass of something else deep-frozen, without destroying or damaging its outside and/or without said outside rotting due to warming up, and refreezing? This is where the theory that the Beresovska mammoth got hit and instantly killed and frozen on the surface—i.e., in air—and was subsequently "buried" breaks down. That it was so, however, is obvious, and, what is more, it is almost as sure that it was frozen first and then buried later, rather than the other way around—vide the perfect condition of its exterior and (don't forget) the little buttercups. The idea that it was first covered with snow and that this then compacted to firn, and thence to ice (glacial type), and finally to palaeocrystic or "fossil" ice, is perfectly splendid; but how then did the muck get in the act? There are only two alternatives: either there never was any snow or ice in the first and second places but an overwhelming tide of muck came along immediately after the elephantine deep-freezing event; or said snow and ice was gradually replaced by muck. But neither of these ideas work either.

First, the thing could not have been overwhelmed by muck because said muck would have also been deep-frozen and therefore of the consistency of a rock. (That it would have had to flow uphill is something else, and a point the advocators of this theory will have to explain). Second, again how did successive floods of muck, warm enough to be plastic, flow uphill, and, more so, how could the outside of the frozen beast—standing presumably now in pristine isolation like a statue due to the warmed temperature which presumably melted all snow and ice—fail to melt and so rot; and when a hairy beast rots from the outside in a moist atmosphere, the first thing that happens is that the outer layer of the skin sloughs off. No, dear experts, these ideas just won't work. You can't have it both ways and you seemingly can't have it either way this time; yet there are the bloody animals to prove that you *must* have it.

I suppose you will say at this point: "OK, you think you're so damned smart, *you* tell us what happened." Well, I can't, and after some thirty years on this bit I don't think I am going to try anymore. There are those that seem to feel I am advocating some kind of cataclysm to account for all these mass deaths, and cataclysms unnerve everybody, let alone scientists. I am not advocating such, though I do think that the suddenly descending globs of supercold air would seem to go further than any other theory to explain the results observable. As to the procedure and process for freezing the stuff I can but rely on the real experts in the meat industry. When it comes to floods of nonfrozen muck running uphill I tend to give up, since I know, as a trained geologist, that the very idea is totally illogical though I suppose nothing is impossible. But getting a solid, deep-frozen elephantine into a solid mass of rock completely buffaloes (or should I say "elephants") me.

Arizona's Great Meteor Crater

Wanda Sue Parrott

When Mount St. Helens erupted in the State of Washington in 1980, the American people were reminded that the North American continent is not nearly as stable a piece of earth as they usually assume. To those who live only in the present, without even an awareness of the San Francisco earthquake of 1906, the idea that U.S. land masses might shift, truly destructive earthquakes take place, or volcanoes erupt, is unimaginable. How much more unimaginable, then, is the idea that a gigantic meteor might strike the earth surface within the continental United States, and leave a huge hole in the ground! But that is precisely what happened in Arizona, just off Highway 66.

An eerie spectacle greets airline passengers flying above the desert of northeastern Arizona if they pass over Winslow shortly before dusk. Then, deepening purple shadows turn the Great Meteor Crater into a huge, toothless mouth that seems to be eternally yawning in the midst of its vast, blank desert face.

The spectacle of the crater is even more intriguing to first-time visitors who drive the long, ribbonlike side road off Highway 66 to get personal glimpses of the cavity which neither time, shifting sands, nor man has obliterated or destroyed. Silence prevails at the site of the crater, with only the occasional mournful sound of wailing winds causing tourists to wonder if the earth is moaning in travail. Those who approach the crater for the first time seem to automatically soften their tones of voice. Often, people speak in whispers as they gaze down into the pit which evokes the remark, "I feel as if I'm witnessing a dead planet."

The site of the crater which draws thousands of tourists each year wasn't always so stark and dry. Today, the giant hole is surrounded by barren, brown-toned land punctuated by a trail of buttes, cones, and volcanic ash residue. The Painted Desert, with its myriad of pastel-hued rock formations, highlights the area northwest of the crater, and the Petrified Forest lies to the east. According to scientific estimates, a magnificent forest once stood in this now-desolate world, but that was around 160 million years ago. Today, all that remains of the flora and fauna of centuries past is rock. Once-majestic plants are now preserved in stone. Yesteryear's trees have turned to agate, and bits and pieces lie as rocks on their dry soil beds.

Visitors must strain their imaginations to envision an aquatic world, teeming with life, on the site where one of the world's still-unresolved mysteries stands. The meteorite which is believed to have caused the crater approximately 20,000 years ago has never been found. However, soil samples taken from the floor of the Great Meteor Crater have yielded bits of shell and other debris left over from an era that preceded man's widespread appearance in this part of the United States.

Scientists conjecture that it was possible that some people did live in the vast valleys of the Southwest by the time the crater was created, but to date no ancient cave drawings or pictographs have been found which offer accounts of what happened during the holocaust that resulted from the meteorite's impact with the earth.

Assuming animals or human beings were present to witness the event, they probably saw a stream of fire pouring down from the sky, perhaps accompanied by a high-pitched, shrill whistle and even a deafening roar. Almost simultaneous with the impact, they witnessed explosions and heat so intense that man could not run fast enough, or animals bury themselves deeply enough, to escape mutilation, incineration, and even instantaneous disintegration.

All that remains to tell the tale of that fateful collision is the crater and meteoritic residue spread across the desert. Since 1871, when white men discovered the crater and believed it to be an extinct volcano, science has attempted to solve the mystery of how the crater was formed and what caused the rain of meteorites that covered an area of at least 550 miles. Currently, it is believed that the same shower of meteorites responsible for the crater in Arizona also caused the Odessa group of craters in Texas.

George Foster, author of *The Meteor Crater Story* (Meteor Crater Enterprises, Inc., Winslow, Arizona), writes of the great crater, "It is now thought that this crater was made some 20,000 years ago, when a huge cluster of meteorites struck from out of the northern sky. It is believed to have weighed at least a million tons and to have been traveling at least several miles per second. It struck at an angle, drove for nearly a mile through solid rock while it was being decelerated to zero velocity, and its fragments finally came to rest below the base of the cliff. . . .

"It is assumed that a cataclysmic explosion occurred as the impacting body was crossing what is now the center of the crater."

Scientific estimates place the speed at which the meteoritic mass was traveling at between 30,000 and 33,000 miles per hour. When the earth was struck with the force of a multi-megaton hydrogen bomb, half a billion tons of rock were displaced. All plant and animal life within a hundred-mile radius are assumed to have been destroyed.

What kind of space "stuff" was responsible for gouging such a hole in earth that the area still bears death scars after 20,000 years? Scientists can only read the elements at hand to gain answers. At the present time, one hypothesis regarding the meteorites which rained down on earth is that the crystal structure indicates many of the meteorites in the shower of 20,000 years ago might be parts of a disrupted planet which possibly once traveled on an orbit located between the orbits of Mars and Jupiter.

That tremendous heat and pressure were present is proved by the composition of the meteorites found around the great crater. Basically, the meteoritic mass from interplanetary space was composed of 92 percent iron, 7 percent nickel, and between 1 and 2 percent minor elements. These included phosphorus, silicon, copper, and carbon, and small amounts of platinum, iridium, cobalt, gold and silver, and even microscopic diamonds. Crystals of silicon carbide, the only natural carborundum ever found on earth, were also present in the meteorites.

How big was the actual meteorite which caused the crater, which is large enough to dwarf the Great Pyramid of Egypt or swallow the Washington Monument? From its rim to its pit bottom, the crater is 570 feet. The diameter of the top of the rim is more than 4,000 feet. A tourist walking around the crater must travel three miles before returning to his starting point. The crater's circumference is approximately a hundredth the circumference of America's largest active volcano, the island of Hawaii. But no one really knows the size of the meteorite that caused it.

E. Opik of Armagh Observatory, Ireland, calculated that the crater was caused by the fall, at about twelve miles per second, of a body approximately two million tons in weight. According to Opik, the meteorite resembled an iron sphere measuring about 260 feet in diameter.

When the rain of meteorites hit, solid rock was literally pulverized, or "splashed," into 300 million tons of material, a third of which has the consistency of powdered sugar or fine flour.

The Great Meteor Crater is the only known crater of its size on earth today which has a meteoritic origin. If other such craters exist, they have been hidden under shifting sands, are overgrown with vegetation, or are located under bodies of water. The true origin of the crater remained a mystery until 1886. Then sheepherders in the desert area found some meteorites about two miles west of the crater.

The discovery of meteorites at the site brought Daniel Moreau Barringer, a mining engineer from Philadelphia, west. In 1902 Barringer acquired the purportedly worthless land and the pit became known as Barringer Crater. The crater was mined, but the ultimate treasure—the great meteorite which caused the phenomenon—was never found. Barringer continued his diggings for thirty years, with only the surface debris in the pit being uncovered.

Although Meteor Crater is not part of the Park Service, it was designated a U.S. Natural Landmark by the Park Service in 1967. In 1971 the designation was changed to National Natural Landmark. The Barringer Crater Company leased the tourist rights at the crater to Meteor Crater . Enterprises, Inc., a corporation formed by the stockholders of Bar T Bar Ranch, Inc., whose lands surrounded the crater. This lease is slated to expire in the year 2157. Currently, thousands of visitors come to the crater site annually. Most of the first-time visitors ask the same questions: What are the chances of another such meteoritic impact with earth happening? How many people would die?

Statistically, odds are small that such a collision, even on a smaller scale, might ever happen again. Since 1790 only twenty-two authenticated cases of meteorites striking and/or damaging buildings have been recorded. But odds are not always accurate, as witnessed by Dr. Lincoln LaPaz of the Department of Mathematics and Astronomy and the Institute of Meteoritics, University of New Mexico.

Back in 1951 Dr. LaPaz calculated that perhaps one person out of three would be struck by a meteorite during this century. A few days after making his statement at a meeting sponsored jointly by the USAF School of Aviation Medicine and the Lovelace Foundation for Medical Education and Research, at San Antonio, Texas, a stony meteorite penetrated the roof of a Sylacauga, Alabama, home. Mrs. E. Hulitt Hodges was stricken while lying down, covered by two quilts. The stone, which ricocheted off the walls, giving her a large bruise on her hip, weighed nine pounds.

A smaller fragment of the meteoritic stone that hit Mrs. Hodges fell several miles distant on the farm of J. K. McKinney.

Small meteorites entering earth's atmosphere would probably burn up before reaching ground level. However, some of the larger meteorites, such as those responsible for the Great Meteor Crater or the Odessa craters or for hitting Mrs. Hughes' home, are large enough to make the trip from space to earth without being consumed.

Meteorites are space debris, according to George Foster, "that has traveled through space, probably through ages of time, until finally they strike the earth's atmosphere. Heat generated by collision with the molecules of the atmosphere vaporizes these particles, and molten material is swept off to make the fiery train we see."

Foster says that generally, since most of the invading particles range in size from a few grains to a fraction of an ounce, vaporization is complete and the flash disappears in an instant of time. A comparative few of greater size survive that flash, at least in part, and strike the earth to supply the only material "from out of this world" that we may see and touch.

Foster's statement was true until a few years ago, when manned and unmanned space flights enabled us to not only photograph interplanetary space and extraterrestrial space bodies, but to bring back to earth some of the stuff from which they are made.

Ironically, the great meteorite which struck earth in approximately 18,000 B.C., then disappeared, leaving in its wake a hole fitting Webster's definition of a crater, "a pit, as one made by a bomb explosion," gave man an initial boost into the realms from where it mysteriously came.

Because the crater strongly resembles the dry, barren surface of the moon, the National Aeronautics and Space Administration established a training ground at the site of the crater. There astronauts learned to walk on the surface of the moon before blasting off from earth.

Bermuda Triangle Mystery

Kent Jordan

For decades, the area popularly known as the Bermuda Triangle has been the scene of a series of mysterious disappearances. Ships of all sizes and types, as well as whole groups of planes, vanished without a trace in an area where the Atlantic Ocean and the Caribbean Sea meet. The disappearance of the SS Marine Sulphur Queen *is one of the best-documented Bermuda Triangle cases. One of the explanations of its fate might be that the vessel simply blew up. But if that happened, floating wreckage and polluted waters ought to have provided ample evidence of such a disaster. Mr. Jordan's account is based on a report of the U.S. Coast Guard's Marine Board of Investigation and its subsequent review by Admiral E.J. Roland, the commandant, U.S. Coast Guard Headquarters, Washington, D.C.*

The SS *Marine Sulphur Queen* left Sabine Sea Buoy at Beaumont, Texas, at 6:30 P.M. on February 2, 1963. The vessel was expected to arrive in Norfolk, Virginia, five days later. It was last heard from on February 4 at 1:25 A.M.

No one knows precisely what happened to the ship, its crew of thirty-nine men, its cargo of 15,260 tons of molten sulphur, or most of its hulk, equipment, and miscellaneous content.

When it became clear, on February 7, that the ship was overdue, the commander of the U.S. Coast Guard's Fifth District notified the Rescue Coordination Center in New York via a "hot line." That same day, an "All Ships Urgent Broadcast" was made for the location and rescue, if possible, of the missing ship. This broadcast was repeated, until February 16. All efforts to contact the vessel by radio were fruitless.

On February 8, at 8:00 A.M., a surface and air search was begun, which followed this pattern:

February 8: A day search was undertaken, following a trackline from Beaumont through the Straits of Florida, a distance of 1,630 miles. Seven planes were used for this search, which covered about 58,000 miles. The search extended thirty miles on either side of the ship's assumed route.

February 8 and 9: Three planes undertook a night search during this period, making twenty-three flights in all and covering 22,000 square miles.

February 9: As the *Marine Sulphur Queen* had not been located on the route, or track, it was supposed to have taken, a much wider search was undertaken. In all, 95,000 miles were covered by nineteen planes, which flew a total number of 114 flight hours.

February 9 and 10: Another night search was undertaken after sunset, with two planes covering 8,300 square miles for a total of twelve flight hours.

February 10: Yet another day search took place. This time, nineteen planes flew 136 hours and searched an area of 76,700 square miles.

February 11: Fourteen planes undertook searches during daylight hours, covering 55,000 square miles in eighty-six flight hours.

February 12: Ten planes flew forty-two hours and searched 22,000 square miles.

February 13: In a final daylight search, two aircraft flew sixteen flight hours and covered an area of 11,000 square miles.

Following this preliminary search in which Coast

Guard, Marine Corps, and Air Force planes participated, it was concluded that the "negative results" indicated further, intensive searches by sea. In all, the planes had flown eighty-three sorties, flying nearly five hundred hours, and covered the vast area of close to 350,000 square miles. Meanwhile, the Coast Guard's Atlantic Merchant Vessel Reporting system got in touch with forty-two ships that could possibly have seen the *Marine Sulphur Queen* during the first days of its voyage. Nothing, however, emerged from these queries that threw any light on the vessel's course or fate.

The Marine Board of Investigation added:

"On 20 February, a U.S. Navy torpedo retriever boat operating about 12 miles southwest of Key West, Florida, sighted and picked up a fog horn and life jacket stenciled with the vessel's name. The second phase of the search for the *Marine Sulphur Queen* was then instituted, confined primarily to the area just west of Dry Tortugas Island, thence through the Straits of Florida, along the axis of the Gulf Stream, including the Bahamas Islands, and the east coast of Florida to Cape Canaveral. This search with seven ships and 48 aircraft sorties flying 271.4 hours covered an additional 59,868 square miles. The probability of sighting during both search phases was computed to be 95 percent for a vessel, 70 percent for a metal lifeboat, and 65 percent for a liferaft.

"The U. S. Navy conducted an underwater search for the vessel's hulk during the period of 20 February through 13 March in an area from the shoals to the 100 fathom curve between Key West and 24°35′N, 83°30′W, using six Navy vessels for 523 hours on the scene and 17 aircraft sorties flying 57 hours with possibility of detection of 80% for the hulk. During this period, additional debris was recovered and identified as coming from the *Marine Sulphur Queen*. At 1740 [5:40 P.M.] EST, 14 March 1963, having received negative reports from all participating units, the search for the vessel was discontinued.

"The material recovered and identified as from the *Marine Sulphur Queen* consisted of 8 life jackets, 5 life rings, 2 name boards, 1 shirt, 1 piece of an oar, 1 storm oil can, 1 gasoline can, 1 cone buoy, and 1 fog horn. This material was deposited with the Coast Guard at Miami, Florida, and later shipped to Washington, D.C., where it was examined by experts from the Bureau of Standards, the Coast Guard, and the Bureau of Fisheries. The consensus of opinion was that possibly two life jackets had been worn by persons and that the shirt tied to a life jacket had also been worn by a person. Numerous tears on the life jackets indicated attack by predatory fish. Further examination was made of certain of the debris by the Federal Bureau of Investigation, who determined that the shirt bore no laundry marks, visible or invisible, and that no trace of sulphur particles was evident on any of the material. Visual examination of the material disclosed no trace of either explosion or fire.

"On 29 April 1963, the Coast Guard Air Detachment, Corpus Christi, was given a note that was reported to have been in a whiskey bottle found on or before that date by a Spanish-speaking man in Laguna Madre, near Corpus Christi at approximate position 29°39.5'N, 97°15.4'W. The bottle was broken to get the note out. A search for pieces of the bottle at that time were negative. However, the Board received the bottom of the purported bottle with no sealife attached thereto on 13 June 1963. This note written with ball point pen on a piece of manila paper, similar to a paper bag, was unsigned and referred to an explosion and two men hurt. The piece of paper also had a crude map of the Gulf of Mexico, Florida Straits and Cuba with a circle surrounding an 'X,' and the word 'SHIP.' This 'X' was near the western approach to the Florida Straits. The note was turned over to a federal examiner of questioned documents who stated in his opinion, based upon crew signatures and a letter from one crew member to his sister, that it was written by a particular crew member."

The bottle, identified with one of the missing crew members, became an elusive element of evidence in locating the vessel and determining the sea and air conditions under which it had operated. The director of the Coast and Geodetic Survey concluded that it could not possibly have reached the Corpus Christi area, assuming it was dropped at any place east of 85 degrees west, "unless a strong southeasterly wind had been blowing for several days before and after the dropping." But winds, at that time, had been northerly.

The Coast Guard investigation concluded that the *Marine Sulphur Queen* had encountered "high and rough seas" on February 3 while in the Gulf of Mexico, and on February 4, while approaching the Straits of Florida. At 1:25 A.M.—in other words, in the early-morning hours—of February 4, the ship transmitted a personal message from a crew member to a shore point; however, near noon the same day, at 11:23 A.M., the ship could no longer be reached by radio, and all later efforts to do so failed. The investigative board concluded that "the vessel foundered sometime on 4 February 1963 on the approach to or in the vicinity of the Straits of Florida." It added, however, that "In view of the absence of any survivors and the physical remains of the vessel, the exact cause for the disappearance of the *Marine Sulphur Queen* could not be ascertained."

Chances are that the vessel exploded in the stormy seas, probably because of structural failures. There wasn't enough time to save the crew, because the few life jackets that were picked up were, the board assumed, probably worn by crew members who were on watch duty and thus "had them readily available." Whatever debris of the vessel was found had been drifting in the waters off the southern tip of Florida. The geodetic report on the message in the bottle made it doubtful that it was dropped into the sea before the vessel foundered—how could anyone have had the time to write the note, put it in the bottle, and tape the bottle shut, when there hadn't even been enough time to send out a radio distress signal?

While the Marine Board of Investigation refers to the assumption that an explosion tore the *Marine Sulphur Queen* apart as "conjecture," it nevertheless indicated such a disaster as a distinct possibility. Its report goes into great detail concerning the construction of the vessel, which had been converted from an oil tanker to a sulphur-carrying vessel in such a way as to weaken it seriously. Divisions between the various sections of the ship had been removed, so that an explosion or other damage occurring in one section of the ship could immediately spread to the rest of the vessel.

Consequently, when Admiral Roland evaluated the board's findings, he noted that, in addition to the explosion hypothesis, it had also been considered that there had been "a complete failure of the vessel's hull girder," which "may have caused it to break in two." Further, the vessel may have "capsized in synchronous rolling" in high seas, or "a steam explosion may have occurred as the result of a rapid filling of the void space with water." The admiral agreed that future oil tankers should not be converted into sulphur tankers in the manner of the *Marine Sulphur Queen*, unless individual cases showed a particularly strong ship's body. After discussing the merits of other recommendations, the admiral stated: "Concurring in another of the board's recommendations, regulations are being developed for submission to the Merchant Marine Council which would require operators of molten sulphur carriers to provide appropriate instructions and indoctrination for vessel personnel concerning hazards of molten sulphur cargoes." The inspection of such ships was to be stepped up, although, since then, few vessels carry molten sulphur.

The case of the SS *Marine Sulphur Queen* is in the category of the "Bermuda Triangle" mysteries only because the Marine Board of Investigation could not decide on the specific cause of the disaster, and because relatively few bits of debris could be found. It is cited by Charles Berlitz in his book *The Bermuda Triangle* in a chapter entitled "The Sea of Lost Ships." Berlitz identifies the last radio message from the vessel as that of a sailor who "had been speculating on the stock market, specifically in wheat futures, a pastime that normally requires rather close contact with one's broker." When the sailor's "buy" order, made before he left Beaumont, could not be confirmed by the brokerage firm—because radio contact could not be established—"the brokerage house informed the ship's owners that they could not reach the vessel." John Wallace Spencer, in *Limbo of the Lost*, summarized the *Marine Sulphur Queen* case factually, but asked: "Why are no lifeboats, oil slick, or floating sulphur found? Why was no distress signal sent?" He added that the boat "was written off" by the Coast Guard inquiry "as just one more un-solved mystery in the 'Limbo of the Lost.'" Richard Winer, in *The Devil's Triangle*, said that as the ship rounded the Florida Keys, "a crew member sent a radio-gram to his wife, telling her of the expected arrival time in Norfolk," while another sailor "sent a radio message to his stockbroker in Tampa." This last reference is presumably another version of the speculation-in-wheat element in the wireless communications to and from the *Marine Sulphur Queen*, although it differs somewhat from Mr. Berlitz' ac-count. Winer noted that almost every article and story on the Bermuda Triangle "includes the loss of the *Marine Sulphur Queen* as a strange mystery," and added that it appeared to be "nothing mysterious or supernatural—sim-ply an industrial explosion at sea." Lawrence D. Kusche, in *The Bermuda Triangle Mystery—Solved*, devotes a chap-ter to the fate of the vessel. After quoting from Coast Guard reports, he wrote that "the legend of the Bermuda Triangle has it that the Coast Guard failed to find an ex-planation for the loss" of the ship, but points out that it listed four possible causes, and the commandant a fifth. Kusche also said:

"Widows and relatives of the men filed suit soon after the incident, asking damages from the owner of the ship. The legal battle has continued for more than ten years. On the tenth anniversary of the *Marine Sulphur Queen*'s dis-appearance it was announced that one of the first of the wrongful death claims had been settled, with court ap-proval of an award of $115,000 to the widow of an ordi-nary seaman. In 1972 the Supreme Court let stand a lower court ruling that the ship was unseaworthy. Claims report-ed to total over $7 million may now be pressed. The rapid sinking of the ship prompted an investigation into the use of automatic emergency warning systems and position-indicating radio beacons."

One reason for paying special attention to the case of the SS *Marine Sulphur Queen*, within the context of the Bermuda Triangle mysteries, is the nature of its disappear-ance, together with the detailed information available concerning the vessel. The farther back an incident, the less reliable information we have; consequently, the more mysterious becomes the disappearance itself. In the case of this sulphur carrier, the data on the condition of the vessel itself are very detailed, and the extensive searches did result in locating such items as life jackets, no matter how few in number. In a sense, then, the *Marine Sulphur Queen* is a "classic" case of what might have been a highly mysterious disappearance—made a good deal less mysterious, although not totally conclusive, by the factual information available.

The Jinx Ship

John Godwin

When the boarding party entered the drifting ship, they found her silent and empty. But the captain's bed was unmade, a bottle of medicine stood opened, and sewing material was neatly laid out for use—all evidence that the ship had been abandoned at a moment's notice. The Mary Celeste had been abandoned, while the sea around her was calm. No evidence of the crew was ever found. In the history of modern navigation the fate of this vessel has remained a mystery. Although doubts have remained, at least a partial answer to the mystery of the Mary Celeste is given in the chapter that follows this narrative.

She was christened *Amazon*. She was listed as British when she was built at Spencers Island, Nova Scotia, in 1861. No one except the keenest of nautical buffs would have recognized her by the name of *Amazon*, for the ship had a second label and flag when she became the classic ocean enigma, eleven years after her launching. Her registry was then American; her name, the *Mary Celeste*.

On the afternoon of December 4, 1872, the British brigantine *Dei Gratia*, out of New York and bound for Gibraltar, had reached a point about 600 miles from the

Portuguese coast when her lookout reported a sail. It turned out to be another brigantine.

The stranger was under short canvas in the brisk northerly wind, yawing heavily while lurching along at a bare two knots. Two of her sheets were missing; the lower foretopsail hung slackly by the corners.

On the *Dei Gratia*, Captain Morehouse and First Mate Oliver Deveau raised their telescopes.

"Why, it's the *Mary Celeste*," exclaimed Morehouse, "and by the looks of it, she's in trouble."

"Seems to be no one at the wheel," said the mate. "Nobody on deck at all. But I don't see any distress signal."

The two ships had now approached within hailing range. Captain Morehouse broke out his speaking trumpet.

"*Celeste* ahoy!" he bellowed. "Can you hear me?"

There was no reply. Just the creaking and flapping of plank and canvas. Morehouse roared again and again, but nothing stirred on the other ship. Only the swish of the waves as the *Celeste* wallowed on, stumbling unevenly, like a blind horse. The captain saw that she was on the starboard tack, but that the jib sail was set to port. To experienced windjammer eyes, this meant only one thing: the ship was out of control, her crew either incapacitated or dead.

Morehouse turned to his first mate. "Mr. Deveau, take two men and board her. Find out what's amiss."

A few minutes later, Deveau and a seaman named Wright were standing on the deck of the *Mary Celeste*. They shouted, stamped their feet, shouted again. No answer . . . only the soft groaning of wood and rope. The wheel stood unattended, spinning idly as the waves slapped at the rudder. The silence was uncanny.

The two men went below and peered into the hold. They searched the galley, the deck cabins, and the forecastle. There wasn't a soul on board. The *Mary Celeste* was a drifter.

But she was a drifter in amazingly good condition. One of Deveau's first acts was to sound the pumps to make sure he hadn't boarded a sinking vessel. There were 40 inches of water in the hold, which meant nothing on a wooden ship. Otherwise, the brig was as tight as a bell, the pumps in prime condition, the rigging neglected but intact, wheel undamaged, not a crack in the planks.

The cargo, consisting of 1,700 casks of undrinkable commercial alcohol, was solidly stowed and in place, though one of the containers had been opened. The only clue to the missing crew was something that *wasn't* there—the lifeboat. The *Celeste*, as Deveau remembered, had carried a yawl lashed to the main hatch. Now the spot was empty. A piece of railing parallel to it had been removed, apparently in order to launch the craft.

The crew, it seemed, had left the ship in the yawl, but they must have left in a feverish hurry. For in the forecastle, the crew had left their sea chests containing their personal possessions, their clothing, oilskins, heavy boots, and most significantly their pipes and tobacco, articles sailors do not abandon unless in fear of death.

In the captain's cabin stood the ship's strongbox safely locked, and the skipper's clock. There were also a few pieces of women's jewelry, a valuable Italian sword, and the logbook. The last entry was dated November 24, and simply recorded the *Celeste*'s position, "about 110 miles due west of the island of Santa Maria in the Azores."

But everything about the vessel's evacuation spelled hurry—hurry—hurry. The captain's bed was unmade; a scrap of paper with an unfinished calculation was lying on the table; loose charts rolled on the floor. A bottle of medicine stood opened, with the cork and spoon lying alongside, as if whoever was about to take it had rushed out in mid-act. In the deck cabin, the skylight stood wide open; and consequently, rain and heavy seas had soaked the bedding, clothing, and shoes and formed large pools on the floorboards.

By way of contrast, all of the cabin's six windows were boarded up with canvas and planks, apparently against heavy seas. Incongruously there was a small phial of sewing-machine oil standing on the table, flanked by a neat array of reels of colored cotton, and some thimbles. Somebody had been preparing to do some sewing when whatever calamity befell the ship interrupted her.

But what calamity? Mate Deveau could find nothing—absolutely nothing—wrong with the vessel. The water below had come in through the open skylight, not through a leak. The pumps worked smoothly and had the water out in a short space of time. There was plenty of food and drinking water in store. Even the missing mainstay sail was found lying on the forward house. Only the foresail and upper foretopsail had been blown from the yards, another indication that the brig had experienced some rough weather.

Captain Morehouse shook his head over his mate's report, but he saw his opportunity. Leaving Deveau and two seamen on board the *Mary Celeste*, he ordered them to follow the *Dei Gratia* into Gibraltar. He would claim the derelict as a salvage prize, his good right—even his duty—but still a very handsome stroke of luck for himself and his company.

The journey to Gibraltar proved a test of the drifter's seaworthiness. The ships struck foul weather that separated them. But the *Celeste* gave her skeleton crew no trouble whatever. She arrived at the British stronghold on December 13, 1872, just twenty-four hours after Morehouse.

The moment she dropped anchor, the vessel was "attached"—meaning impounded—by the marshal of the Vice-Admiralty Court, prior to the hearing of the salvage claim. And almost immediately, the official atmosphere grew distinctly chilly.

According to international maritime law, salvagers acquire a lien on property they recover through their efforts. In most cases, a salvaged vessel is a partial or complete wreck, left as a dead loss by the original crew. Here, however, the craft in question was an eminently seaworthy ship, whose cargo alone was valued at around $30,000. Why, then, had it been abandoned?

The British naval authorities sent two divers down to inspect the *Celeste* below the waterline. They detailed one shipwright, two carpenters, three Royal Navy captains, the local shipping surveyor, and a timber expert to go through every rib and beam of the vessel in search of some flaw that might have caused her evacuation. They found nothing except signs of normal wear and tear. If anything, the *Mary Celeste* was in better all-round condition than the majority of small cargo craft plying the North Atlantic.

And yet, as the skipper, mate, and the entire crew of the *Dei Gratia* asserted in unison, they had come upon this amply provisioned brigantine drifting unmanned in mid-ocean. Odd—very, *very* odd!

Now there came upon the scene Her Majesty's Advocate-General and Proctor for the Queen in her office of Admiralty, and Attorney-General for Gibraltar, one Solly Flood. Mr. Flood was an excitable little man of unsquelchable pomposity, towering bathos, and considerable shrewdness. He was also a painstaking investigator, a legal bloodhound of the stripe who would rather see ten innocent men hanged than a single guilty one escape. Mr. Flood convinced himself that he was dealing with a case of piracy and multiple murder.

Foul play *must* have taken place. How else could the crew of the *Dei Gratia* have gained possession of a perfectly sound ship? And in order to substantiate his notion, Mr. Flood was ready if not to move mountains, then at least to juggle the evidence.

He ascertained the fact that the two ships had lain in New York Harbor at the same time before their departures. He also discovered—and this struck him as particularly suspicious—that the two skippers knew each other well and had had dinner together before leaving New York. "Captain Morehouse, therefore, was familiar with the strength of the crew as well as the value of the *Mary Celeste*'s cargo," he proclaimed, his tone hinting that this unremarkable fact somehow indicated piratical intent.

Then, during the proceedings before the Admiralty Court, Solly Flood unrolled the strands from which he hoped to twist a rope for the necks of the *Dei Gratia* crew.

There was, the Advocate-General asserted, a deep cut in the starboard rail of the ship, a notch such as must have been inflicted by the blow of a sharp instrument. Had Mr. Deveau noticed that? The mate replied that he hadn't. The relevant piece of railing was brought into court.

There was a brown spot on the deck near the cut, Mr. Flood went on, a spot which *might* have been blood. Did Mr. Deveau, by any chance, have the deck scraped?

"I didn't notice any blood on deck," said the mate.

"And we never washed or scraped the deck of the *Mary Celeste*. We didn't have the time. But the sea washed over the deck."

"Salt water," Mr. Flood announced ominously, "contains chloric acid which dissolves blood particles."

Having driven home this point, the Advocate-General proceeded. Had Mr. Deveau seen the Italian sword aboard the *Mary Celeste*?

"Yes, I found that sword under the captain's berth," the mate replied. "I looked at it by drawing it from its sheath. Then I put it back where I found it, or somewhere near. There was nothing remarkable about it. It seemed rusty."

"That sword," Mr. Flood thundered, "has been cleaned with lemon, which covered it with citrate of iron. Therefore, another substance was put there to disguise the original marks of blood which were once there!"

Having found no bloodstains on either the deck or the sword blade, the legal eagle was trying to make a case out of an assumption that bloodstains *might* have once been on the deck and the sword.

But these were merely random shots. Flood's broadsides were still to come. He seized on the last entry in the derelict's log, which placed her off Santa Maria Island on November 24, heading northeast. According to their statements, the crew of the *Dei Gratia* had sighted the *Celeste* ten days later, about 550 miles farther on than Santa Maria, and the *Celeste* was still heading northeast. How, Mr. Flood asked, was it possible for an unmanned ship with a loose wheel and the wind blowing steadily from the north to have maintained her course over such a time and distance? The implication was clear: the *Dei Gratia* must have met and boarded the *Celeste* much earlier than they said they had.

Mate Deveau was quite unable to clear up that point. All he could do was surmise that the drifter might have changed directions several times in the meanwhile. He grew even more uncomfortable when the Advocate-General inquired whether he had kept the salvaged ship's log up to date from the time he sailed her, as required by law.

"Yes, I kept the log after I got on board," said the mate

hesitantly, "—that is to say, I wrote it out by memory after we got into Gibraltar."

"My own theory," thundered Solly Flood, "is that the crew got at the alcohol, and in the fury of drunkenness murdered the master, his wife and child, and the chief mate; that they then damaged the bows of the vessel with the view of giving it the appearance of having struck on the rocks, so as to induce the master of any vessel which might pick them up, if they saw her at some distance, to think her not worth attempting to save; and that they did, some time between the 25th November and the 5th December, escape on board some vessel bound for some North or South American port of the West Indies."

Before a jury of landlubbers, Mr. Flood might have boxed the *Dei Gratia's* crew into a corner. Luckily for them, he was performing before a naval court and judge. For all their pettifogging slowness, these gold-braided seadogs knew more about windjammers than did the Advocate-General, enough to realize that the points he had so elaborately made weren't worth a pinch of snuff.

The deep cut in the starboard railing could have been made by any sailor hacking a rope. The cleaning job on the sword blade had, in all probability, been done by the skipper of the *Celeste* himself. If the weapon had really shown bloodstains, the man who wished to eliminate such evidence would have simply thrown it overboard.

The sailing feat of the unmanned brig had an equally simple explanation. Mr. Flood had assumed that the last entry in the log meant that the *Mary Celeste* must have been abandoned the same day. Actually, many small merchant vessels did not make daily log entries, the court pointed out, frequently missing three or four days unless something of importance occurred. The evacuation of the *Celeste*, therefore, could have happened much later than November 24, which would reduce the span of her unmanned run.

The court also concluded that the cargo alcohol was quite undrinkable. If the men had quaffed the stuff, they would have been rolling around in convulsions instead of murdering their officers.

Finally, the court refused to attach any sinister motives

to the fact that Deveau had written up the log of the salvage prize in retrospect. Having only two men with which to work a vessel that normally required seven and being unfamiliar with the ship, Deveau could hardly have had time for much paperwork en route.

The naval authorities were fairly prompt in clearing Morehouse and his men of any suspicion. But they spent months trying to formulate an official explanation for what had happened to the *Celeste*. They drove her American owner into a roaring fury with their demands for more detailed information about the ship, her crew, her skipper, her history, and himself, grilling him to the stage where he barked: "I'm a Yankee with some English blood, but if I knew where it was, I'd open a vein and let the damned stuff out!"

They queried every port within reach for news of possible survivors. They solicited the opinions of American marine brokers, Canadian ship builders, and British naval experts. They consulted meteorologists, zoologists, and criminologists. They questioned London's venerable Lloyd's Corporation for cases of precedence. But their efforts produced no satisfactory answer—in fact, no answer at all. When, in March 1873, the court finally handed down its judgment, it did so without expressing an opinion—the first time in its existence it had ever refrained from offering one. The decision awarded 1,700 pounds (about $8,300) to the *Dei Gratia*, roughly one-fifth of the combined value of the salvaged ship and her cargo.

The *Mary Celeste* was handed back to her Yankee owner. She got a new captain, and a new crew, and she sailed on to Genoa, where she discharged her cargo—perfectly intact but three and a half months late. Over her loomed an invisible but ever-present question mark that cast a shadow nobody has ever been able to lift—what had happened to the *Mary Celeste* on that stretch of water between the Azores and the coast of Portugal?

It would be just as pertinent to ask what had been happening to her from the moment her keel touched salt water. For if ever a ship carried a jinx, it was the *Mary Celeste*, née *Amazon*, and she carried that curse up to the moment of her death.

There is a universal sailors'. superstition about "ships born unlucky," and such a hoodoo has certainly applied to particular ships. One thinks of the *Great Eastern*, of England's *Hood*, and of Nazi Germany's *Tirpitz*. And surely a jinx haunted the *Celeste* without letup from the day of her baptism on.

She began life as a British brigantine in Nova Scotia, Canada, an all-wood 282-tonner, 103 feet long, 25 feet across the beam, with very comfortable deck houses. She was registered as the *Amazon*. Forty-eight hours later, her skipper died. On her maiden voyage, she ran into a fishing weir off the coast of Maine, which put a severe gash in her hull. While still under repair, fire broke out amidship. This cost her second captain his job. It was under her third commander that she crossed the Atlantic for the first time—and promptly collided with another vessel in the Straits of Dover. Repaired once again—and with yet a fourth skipper—she returned to Canada. There, in November 1867, she ran aground on Cape Breton Island and became a wreck.

At this point, the history of her ownership grows somewhat murky. She was salvaged by either a Mr. Haines or an Alexander McBean—accounts differ—but either or both of these gentlemen went bankrupt almost immediately, and the hulk passed into the possession of one John Beatty of New York, who, in his turn, sold the *Amazon* to another New York ship owner, James H. Winchester.

In the process, the ship acquired a different name and nationality as well as a new structure. For reasons unknown, Winchester rechristened her the *Mary Celeste*. Now she flew the Stars and Stripes instead of the Red Ensign, had a brand-new copper-lined bottom, and an extended deck cabin. Her underwriters, the Atlantic Mutual Insurance Company, passed her as "well built and sea worthy." But there were any number of seamen who refused to sail on her. An unlucky maiden voyage *and* a change of name was a combination almost as ill-starred as the shooting of an albatross.

The ship's fifth master was also part owner. Captain Benjamin Spooner Briggs, from Marion, Massachusetts, was as straight-laced a puritanical gentleman as ever left

New England. He stood in striking contrast to the hard-swearing, semiliterate Winchester. At thirty-eight, Briggs was a stern-featured, slightly stuffy man of few words, who placed a harmonium on board the vessel, read a Bible chapter aloud every evening, and said "durn" when he meant "damn."

Captain Briggs took along his wife, Sarah Elizabeth, and their baby daughter, by no means an unusual act in those days of long voyages. As first and second mates, he had two Yankees, Albert G. Richardson and Dane Andrew Gilling. New Yorker Albert Head came as sea cook. The four seamen—Goodschad, Lorenzen, Martens, and Volkert—were of German birth. It was a good, solid ship's company, every one a man of spotless reputation, and morally at least several cuts above the average windjammer crew.

Early in November 1872, the *Mary Celeste* lay at Pier 44 in New York's East River, where she was being loaded with a cargo of commercial alcohol destined for Genoa, Italy. Nearby lay the brigantine *Dei Gratia*, taking on a mixed cargo for Gibraltar. Her skipper, David Reed Morehouse, was an old friend of Captain Briggs. Their wives knew each other, too. Two nights before his departure, Briggs dined with his fellow-captain at the Astor House and they wished each other fair winds. They were never to meet again.

Briggs seemed happy about his crew. "They are all good and willing fellows," he remarked, "but I have yet to find out how smart they are."

With his vessel in fine sailing trim, the bewhiskered, pious, teetotaling captain embarked from New York on November 5. Because of severe headwinds, he anchored off Staten Island for two days, and then set out into the North Atlantic.

The *Dei Gratia* left on November 11. Twenty-three days later, the two ships met in midocean, an encounter that scriptwriters have been embellishing ever since.

After she was found unmanned, interest in what had happened to the *Celeste* grew only gradually. Brief notice was taken at the time of the proceedings before the Gibraltar Admiralty Court. It was over the years that the story gained in bulk, developing an avalanche of books, articles, poems, radio dramas, films, and television features. For the *Celeste* turned into a universal guessing game. A few dramatic touches were added, of course: her tables were set with uneaten food; an all-revealing page was missing from the log book; Briggs was a religious maniac; his crew were professional cutthroats.

In 1884, Conan Doyle wrote a blood-drenched little romance called "J. Habakuk Jephson's Statement" relating the fate of the "Marie (sic) Celeste." Unbeknown to contemporaries, she had carried an exceedingly ambitious colored passenger named Septiminus Goring who proceeded to slaughter every soul on board in order to seize the ship and with it establish his own black empire in Africa. Doyle at least disguised his brainchild as semi-fiction. Those who followed his path unblushingly proclaimed theirs as revelations.

Around 1900 came a spate of "monster-from-the-depths" accounts. Some of these tales recounted how the brigantine had been attacked by a kraken, a devil fish or giant squid, which picked up the crew rather as a gourmet picks snails from their shells, reaching its tentacles through the portholes until the last human morsel had gone. After which it presumably swallowed the yawl by mistake.

In 1926, the Englishman Adam Bushey suggested that the *Celeste* had been "dematerialized" en route. If one follows Bushey's logic, the people who sailed on the *Celeste* remained, well, dematerialized, while the ship itself returned to its solid form.

Charles Fort—the world's foremost interpreter of unsubstantiated newspaper clippings—hinted that the missing crew and passengers could have been whisked away by what he termed a "selective force," a force that left the ship itself untouched. He didn't say where the people had been whisked *to*, but then Fort rarely concerned himself with trivialities.

In 1955, UFO expert Professor Jessup came up with the unchallengeable hypothesis that the company was snatched away by a flying saucer. Since UFOs have been accused of purloining anything from Texan cows to lady realtors, there is no reason why they shouldn't have indulged in a spot of marine kidnapping, too.

Although nothing was actually ever heard again from any known member of the ship's company, there was a steady surfacing of *Mary Celeste* survivors whose names, somehow, had been left out of the ship's register. They popped up in all localities, with stories that ranged from the ridiculous to the imbecilic.

In 1913, the *Strand Magazine* of London published the adventures of one such survivor, yclept Abel Fosdyk. Mr. Fosdyk had it that the crew and passengers were drowned while watching a swimming race around the ship between the captain and the mate. For this purpose, they had built a platform under the bow (hence the scratches), which collapsed under their combined weight. All perished except the author, who saved himself on a raft.

Only one unprovable yet feasible solution has ever been advanced—unprovable because no witnesses are available. This one theory takes into account all of the verified circumstances.

According to the evidence, three salient facts emerge: (1) The ship was abandoned in great haste; (2) Those who abandoned ship did so in the ship's yawl; (3) The abandonment took place under responsible guidance, since the chronometer, the sextant, the navigation books, and the ship's papers were missing and in all probability had been taken along.

Since the vessel had sustained no structural damage, the cause of her evacuation was not something that *had* happened, but something that seemed *about* to happen. The only danger potential at the time was her cargo.

Captain Briggs had never carried crude alcohol before, and was likely unfamiliar with its chemical reactions. He had come from wintry New York to the much warmer region of the Azores; and the barrels—severely shaken by stormy weather—might have exuded vapors. One of the barrels, it will be remembered, had been opened—probably in the course of a cargo inspection. If this inspection had taken place with a naked light, there might have been something of a slight explosion—too slight to inflict damage, but loud enough to convince the skipper that the whole cargo was about to blow sky-high.

The presence on board of his wife and baby daughter may have raised Captain Briggs' fear to panic level, and he precipitously ordered all hands into the lifeboat.

In all likelihood, the captain intended to stick close enough to his ship to get back on, if no further explosion occurred. But for safety's sake, he couldn't linger *too* close. Then—with a gust of wind—came tragedy! The *Mary Celeste* sailed away from the little craft.

The rest is easily imagined—the men rowing with the strength of despair—the distance increasing inexorably—finally exhaustion—and the ship gliding out of sight.

There was no land closer than three or four hundred miles, and during the next few days, a single wave could have swamped the yawl.

This theory was first offered by James Winchester, the ship's owner at the time. This hypothesis was later expanded by several authors, but somehow has never found general acceptance. Mutineers, pirates, ocean monsters, unknown forces, and man-snatching saucers were so-o-o-o much more exciting.

Winchester got rid of the ship as soon as she arrived back in New York, some say at a dead loss. But this seems improbable from what we know of Winchester. The man who took the real loss was her unlucky purchaser, for the jinx that lurked in the *Celeste*'s very timbers remained as potent as ever.

The new owner loaded the *Celeste* with a cargo of lumber and dispatched her to Montevideo. En route, in a storm, she lost her entire deck cargo and a good part of her rigging, a loss severe enough to knock any profit out of the journey. On the return trip, carrying a load of horses and mules, most of the living cargo died in the hold; and a few days later, her new skipper followed suit.

From then on, the *Celeste* changed hands so fast and frequently that it becomes almost impossible to keep track of who owned her and when. Ships in those days of lax safety regulations were kept in service until they literally fell apart, and ownership was frequently split among twenty or more part owners. This seems to have been the fate of the aging *Mary Celeste*—lurching up and down the American coastline, shedding spars, sails, and sailors, scraping on sandbanks, catching fire—but still holding together, still running sweet if well handled, still piling on mishap after mishap.

Then, in 1884, she fell into the hands of a grizzled sea shark named Gilman C. Parker, another Massachusetts man, but not of the teetotaling kind. For most of his sixty-one years, Captain Parker had dabbled in every brand of nautical skulduggery, except outright piracy. Now he and a group of dryland buccaneers hatched a scheme to wring a fat profit out of the notoriously unprofitable *Celeste*. They loaded her with a cargo of junk, worth but a few hundred dollars, but registered the cargo as high-class merchandise and managed to insure the ship for $27,000. Then Captain Parker took the *Celeste* on her death ride to the Caribbean.

In the Haitian Gulf of Gonave lies a coral reef named Rochelois Bank that looks like a row of teeth which were especially designed to tear wooden ships to shreds. Parker set course for that reef and he ordered his helmsman to stay on it. The brigantine ground into the razorlike coral, and with the waves crashing around her, began to settle.

There was no imminent danger, for the ship stuck high and dry. The crew had ample time to row the cargo ashore. When everything sellable had been salvaged, Parker ordered kerosene sprinkled over the deck, and he then lit the torch. Under the hot sun, the *Celeste* turned into a roaring pyre. That evening nothing remained of her save her charred ribs.

Back in Boston, Parker and associates filed their claim. The insurance companies, however, smelled a herd of rats, and dispatched their detectives to quiz the crew. The sailors talked; the investigators took notes. In due time, Captain Parker and three of his partners faced a federal court in Boston on a charge of barratry—a hanging crime in those days.

But it was the jury which was hung instead of the defendants. The four conspirators walked out of the court scot-free, but they couldn't collect their claim, and the notoriety killed their credit. Eight months later, Parker died in disrepute and poverty. One of his associates was consigned to a lunatic asylum; another committed suicide. Within a year, the two companies involved in the swindle went bankrupt.

Even after her immolation, the most famous bad-luck ship in history affected all connected with her.

The Mary Celeste
Mystery—Solved?

Dr. Oliver W. Cobb

If the reader has seen the preceding chapter, "The Jinx Ship," he will have a detailed picture of the mysterious image that has developed around the derelict vessel Mary Celeste. *But was the fate of that ship really all that inexplicable? Can a rational explanation, or series of explanations, account for the ship's condition? The magazine* Yachting, *which originally published Dr. Cobb's analysis of the vessel's fate, observed that few cases have "intrigued the imagination of people, both ashore and afloat," as much as "the fate and the captain of the brig* Mary Celeste *when that vessel was sighted and boarded south and west of the Azores in the year 1872." The magazine added that Oliver Cobb's reconstruction of events came from "a relative and contemporary of the captain of the brig and his wife, a seafaring man himself, and the facts he presents are those accepted in the family, by the agent for the vessel in New York, and by marine underwriters."*

Because of my personal knowledge of and relation to Captain Benjamin S. Briggs and his wife Sarah Everson (Cobb), who were cousins of mine, and my long acquaintance with their families, I feel compelled to write the story of the loss of the brig *Mary Celeste* and shed some much needed light on the so-called mystery surrounding the disappearance of the captain and crew of that vessel. I desire to get before the reading public the truth so far as we know it regarding the fate of those who were on board the *Mary Celeste*, November 24, 1872.

The story is founded on my personal knowledge, the record of the Admiralty Court at Gibraltar, the letters of Mr. Sprague (the American Consul at Gibraltar), the family records at Marion, Massachusetts, and the inscriptions on the monument on the Briggs burial lot in the Evergreen Cemetery at Marion.

In 1863, Captain Benjamin S. Briggs married Sarah Everson Cobb. He was then in command of the three-masted schooner *Forest King* and for their honeymoon he took his wife with him on a voyage to Mediterranean ports. Later, Captain Briggs commanded the bark *Arthur* and Sarah continued to sail with him until 1865, when she came home to Marion and a son, Arthur, was born to them at Rose Cottage, the home of the Briggs family. After this event, Mrs. Briggs continued to sail with her husband in the *Arthur* and later in the brig *Sea Foam*. On one of these voyages they were at Fiume, Austria, where Captain Briggs picked up a sword with the cross of Navarre on the hilt. This sword later appears on board the *Mary Celeste*.

In the summer of 1872, on my return from a voyage to the Mediterranean in the brig *Julia A. Hallock*, I was again at Rose Cottage, Marion. Captain Ben and Sarah, now with two children, lived next door. At this time, Captain Briggs was looking for a business on shore as he wished to be with his family. As he found nothing but the sea to satisfy him, he bought the brig *Mary Celeste* and, as his wife was ready to go with him, he had some changes made in the arrangement of the cabin in order to make things more convenient for her. Sarah took along her sewing machine and her melodeon. The brig was chartered for the Mediterranean with a full cargo consisting of 1,700 barrels of alcohol, valued at about $38,000. They expected to be very comfortable. I well remember the plans for this voyage. Captain Ben told Sarah that Mr. Richardson was going with him as mate; he had been with Captain Briggs before this. They were taking their younger child, Sophia

Matilda, now two years old, with them and leaving Arthur, now seven, to live with his grandmother so that he might go to school. The *Mary Celeste* cleared from the Custom House at New York, November 7th, 1872, with the following on board: Captain Benjamin S. Briggs, Mate Albert G. Richardson, Second Mate Andrew Gilling, Cook E. W. Head, Seamen Volkert Lorenzeau, Arien Harens, Bos Larensen, Gottlieb Goodschoad, and the captain's wife and two-year-old daughter.

A little less than a month later, on December 4th, 1872, Captain Morehouse of the British brig *Dei Gratia*, on her way to Gibraltar, saw the *Mary Celeste* headed westerly with a northerly wind with but three sails set. As it was evident to him that something was wrong with the vessel, he sent his mate, Mr. Deveau, to investigate.

Mr. Deveau found no one on board. The yawl boat was gone. The boat had been carried across the main hatch and, as the section of the rail abreast the hatch had been taken out and lay on deck, it was evident that the boat had been launched from the port side.

The fore hatch lay upside down on deck. The upper topsail and the foresail had blown away. The lower topsail, jib and foretopmast staysail were set. All other sails were furled except that the main staysail was loose on top of the forward house. Water was in the forward house, sloshing about up to the sill. Some water was found between decks, and three and one half feet of water in the lower hold. There had evidently been some water in the cabin as some things there were wet. The beds were made and there was what appeared to be the impress of a child's head on the pillow of the captain's bed.

The log book lay open on the mate's desk and the last entry reads: "Weather, fine: wind, light; St. Mary's Island distant about six miles. Latitude 37° N, longitude 25° 02″ W." And the date: November 24th, 1872. St. Mary's Island mentioned was evidently Santa Maria, the southeasterly island of the Azores group. On the book lay a sheet of paper on which Mr. Richardson had begun a letter to his wife. He had written only four words, "Fannie My Dear Wife. . . ." Evidently he wanted to have a letter ready to mail on arrival at Gibraltar. If he had only written a few more words, his letter might possibly have shed some light on the story of the *Mary Celeste.*

We are quite dependent upon the evidence of the salvors as we try to construct the story. We must be mindful of the fact that Mr. Deveau and the two sailors who with him brought the *Mary Celeste* to Gibraltar, where they went into the Admiralty Court suing for salvage compensation, were coached by an attorney, and it was or seemed to be to their advantage to make the situation or condition as bad for the vessel as possible. I suspect that there was some "window dressing." There must have been some reason why Captain Morehouse of the *Dei Gratia* stipulated that he was not to be called into court.

It is interesting to read the evidence given by these men. They all say that the lower topsail was "hanging by the four corners." It always did depend on those four corners except that.it would have rope yarn rovings securing the head of the sail to the jackstay on the yard. One man says that all the cabin windows were covered with canvas and boards nailed on outside. Another said the windows on one side only were like this and he was very sure there was only glass in the other windows. One was sure that the standing rigging was in good shape while another said that it needed much work to put it in order. All said that the binnacle which had been between two cleats on top of the house was displaced and the compass broken. One said that the cleats were broken, but the man who replaced the binnacle said that the cleats were all right and that the binnacle slipped in between the cleats and that it was only perhaps ten minutes' work to replace it. A spare compass was found in the cabin. Much was said about the water in the hold, between decks, and in the forward house. Some things were wet in the cabin. Now, three and one half feet of water in an empty hold would be quite a bit of water but in a hold filled with barrels closely packed and chocked with wood it means comparatively little water. Very little water would remain between decks. As to the water in the forward house, the door of which was open, if even a moderate sea came on deck it could easily slop over the sill into the galley and stay there. The fore hatch being off, any quantity of water that was shipped would go into the hold. As the doors of the forward companionway to the cabin were open, some water would be likely to get into the cabin.

Contrary to many reports, there was no cooked food found on board the vessel but enough provisions to last her crew for six months.

One man said that there was no sign of a boat being carried across the main hatch, and another said that certain rough timbers lashed across the hatch showed beyond a doubt that the boat had been carried there. One man said that "the peak halliards were gone"; another that "they were broken and gone." And yet no one seems to have thought that when the boat left the vessel the peak halliards might have been taken as a tow rope.

As the entry in the log book made at noon, November 24th, indicates light southerly wind, the *Mary Celeste* was then probably under full sail. This enables us to reconstruct what probably happened. At some time after noon of November 24th, Captain Briggs determined to take in sail. He may have interrupted Mr. Richardson's letter writing. The royal and topgallant sail, the flying jib, main topmast staysail, middle staysail, gaff topsail and the mainsail were furled.

The vessel was still on the starboard tack as is shown by the jibs being set on the port side. That the yards were braced around so as to back the squaresails is evident from the position of the yards when the salvors went on board. The movable section of the rail abreast the main hatch had been taken out and laid on deck where Mr. Deveau said that he left it until he went on board the second time. All the above movements indicate good seamanship and preparation to leave the vessel. We do not know why, but I think that the cargo of alcohol, having been loaded in cold weather at New York early in November and the vessel having crossed the Gulf Stream and being now in comparatively warm weather, there may have been some leakage and gas may have accumulated in the hold. The captain, having care for his wife and daughter, was probably unjustifiably alarmed and, fearing a fire or an explosion, determined to take his people in the boat away from the vessel until the immediate danger should pass.

Knowing what the duty of each man would be, it is comparatively easy to reconstruct the scene with the evidence which we have. The boat was launched on the port side. The captain got his wife and daughter into the boat, and left them in charge of Mr. Richardson with one sailor in the boat while the captain went for his chronometer, sextant, *Nautical Almanac* and the ship's papers.

Mr. Gilling with one sailor would be getting the peak halliard ready to use as a tow rope. Another sailor would tend the painter of the boat and a fourth sailor would be at the wheel. The cook gathered up what cooked food he had on hand and some canned goods.

There is some evidence of haste in the act of leaving the vessel. The sailors left their pipes. The main staysail was not furled. The wheel was left loose. The binnacle was displaced and the compass broken, probably in a clumsy attempt to get the compass quickly.

It may well have been that just at that time came an explosion which might have accounted for the fore hatch being upside down on deck, as found. It was currently reported at the time that the captain left his watch and money in his desk and that money was found in the sailors' chests by the salvors—probably small sums of money if any, and the captain's watch probably became a keepsake for somebody. These articles do not appear in the court record and are not mentioned in the memorandum of personal effects which Mr. Sprague, the American Consul, submitted.

Whatever happened, it is evident that the boat with ten people in her left the vessel and that the peak halliard was taken as a tow line and as a means of bringing the boat back to the *Mary Celeste* in case no explosion or fire had destroyed the vessel. Probably a fresh northerly wind sprang up, filled the square-sails and the vessel gathered way quickly. The peak halliard, made fast at the usual place on the gaff, would be brought at an acute angle across the bulwarks at the gangway. With the heavy boat standing still at the end, I do not wonder that the halliard parted. This would tally exactly with the evidence given in court that "the peak halliard was broken and gone." This fact was impressed upon the sailors as they had to get up a coil of rope from the lazarette and reeve off a new peak halliard before they could set the mainsail.

When the tow rope parted, these people were left in an open boat on the ocean as the brig sailed away from them. The wind that took the vessel away may have caused sea enough to wreck them. They perished—let us hope quickly. Nothing has appeared in all these sixty-seven years to tell us of their end. What we know and can surmise from the facts has been told here.

The sword with the cross of Navarre on the hilt, which "Frederick Solly Flood, Esquire, Advocate, and Proctor for the Queen in Her Office of Admiralty" at Gibraltar sought to prove had been used for some nefarious purpose, was not listed by the American Consul among the effects of Captain Briggs. It remained on board the *Mary Celeste* until after a subsequent voyage when George Orr took it home with him to Rerton, N. B. I am told that the sword is still in the family of Captain Orr, at Rerton.

The *Mary Celeste* was built at Spencer Island and registered at Parrsboro, N.S., as the *Amazon*, a single-deck vessel with cabin and forward house on deck, a half-brig rig with a large single topsail. The first captain died three days after he took command. A year later, in 1862, she was at Marseilles, France, and a painting of the vessel was made. This picture is now owned by Mr. R. Lester Dewis, of West Advocate, N.S.

In 1867 the *Amazon* was wrecked in Glace Bay, Newfoundland. As Glace Bay was prohibited by the insurance people and the cost of refloating seemed to be excessive, the owners abandoned her to the salvors. The brig was finally floated, sold to American owners, taken to an American port, an upper deck was added, the forward house raised to stand on the upper deck, a lower topsail yard was added, dividing the topsail. The name was changed to *Mary Celeste* and she was given American registry. The above changes had increased her tonnage measurement from 198.42 to 268 tons.

Captain Briggs bought this vessel in the fall of 1872, and you have read the story of his disaster.

In the following two or three years, the *Mary Celeste* made various voyages and finally was loaded with a cargo of doubtful value on which excessive insurance had been placed. The vessel was wrecked on the coast of Haiti under suspicious circumstances. The insurers refused to pay and charged the captain with *barratry*. For various reasons, the trial was postponed. Two years passed and the captain died, not having been brought to trial.

The Monster of Loch Ness

W. R. Akins

Among ancient traditions that have retained a hold on our time, the image of giant animals is perhaps the most picturesque. We are somehow not satisfied with mere drawings of such prehistoric animals as the dinosaur, or with the giant skeletons that can be found in museums. Somehow, man retains a fascination for "the real thing"—a giant creature that has somehow survived the vicissitudes of evolution. We are impressed with the size and survival powers of the whale, and we seek other giant animals, perhaps descendants of dragons, in the world's waters. Mr. Akins, author of the The Loch Ness Monster (Signet, 1977), presents an up-to-date account of the elusive creature which may or may not be native to Scotland.

I

Any realm of the gods must have its devils; the more powerful and virtuous the former, the more terrifying and evil the latter. Of all these demons, those of the sea are the most monstrous, huge, repulsive, and destructive. The existence of these aquatic monsters has haunted man since antiquity, and at times with truth, as in the case of the legendary *kraken*, which proved to be the giant squid. Could

81

the "monster" in Loch Ness similarly turn out to be real? Before we look at the facts in the matter and try to answer the question, let us look briefly at its origin in myth and legend.

Though most people nowadays associate the dragon with fire, his primeval element was water, whether the sea, rivers, lakes like Scotland's Loch Ness, waterspouts or rainclouds. This watery connection chiefly distinguishes the dragon, or sea serpent, from other mythical hybrids. Even the desert-dwelling people insist on it, and their dragons spend a lot of time lurking at the bottom of wells.

This transition of the dragon from a watery to a fiery creature may seem strange, but like all creatures, both mythical and real, it has evolved. It is possible that the remains of giant saurians inspired man to his earliest stories about monsters. Among extant creatures, however, the dragon's earliest identifiable progenitor is the serpent, and some authorities believe that they can trace the lineage of dragons all over the world back to one common ancestor, Zu, the monster of watery chaos in Sumerian mythology.

The Sumerians settled in Mesopotamia in the fifth millennium B.C., and their struggle to tame the rivers in that country inspired several myths. Their most important god was Enlil, who started life as a river god, but moved on to dry land and the upper world. The serpent or dragon Zu stole the tablets worn by Enlil on his chest, on which were engraved the laws which governed the universe. On Enlil's orders, Zu was slain by the sun god Ninurta, who thus set the precedent for sun gods who battle with monsters in other ancient myths.

The Sumerians were superseded, about 1800 B.C., by the Babylonians, a Semitic people who inherited many of their beliefs. They continued the association of water gods with chaos, and the connection is not hard to see. It seems likely that Babylonian or Sumerian influences were at work from an early period in Egypt. The dragon or water-monster myth is thought to have reached there toward the end of the third millennium B.C.

The process by which different peoples develop and adapt a vague concept in a way which suits their own needs and experience can be traced in the treatment of the sea-serpent myth. The gigantic serpent of the Egyptians, Apophis (or Apep, Apop), was identified with the ocean which girded the world and held it together, but also threatened to break its fetters and destroy the world. At a later period, the dragon was identified with the god Seth, violent "Lord of the South," god of earthquakes, hurricanes, thunder, and destructions, who shook the very sea itself. In the oldest writings in the Old Testament, Yahweh is represented as a storm god, at whose coming "the earth trembled, and the heavens dropped, yea, the clouds dropped water, the mountains quake before the Lord."

Jewish writings of the first century A.D. depict the sea serpent as a symbol of mourning and desolation. In early Christian texts, the serpent or dragon represents the devil, an identification suggested by the leathery webbed feet and forked tail common to both, in line with the conception of the dragon as the enemy or adversary of saints and the Divine.

The dragon is described as a three-headed creature in the earliest mention of him in ancient Greek literature, Homer's *Iliad*; Agamemnon's sword belt is decorated with a blue enamel dragon and there are three dragons on his cuirass.

Another peculiarly Greek idea is that of the dragon's connection with treasure, which first appears in the dream interpretations of Artemidoros (second century A.D.), wherein we are told dragons make their "fixed abode" over treasure.

The association between dragons, caves, and treasure, reinforced by the Teutonic myth of the dragon Fafnir, became very popular in the early Christian period and the later Middle Ages, especially in the legend of St. George. In the original Teutonic myth, Fafnir lurks in a cave, watching over a treasure hoard which is the source of life and power (in Christian thought, the treasure is the mystical communion with God). Siegfried is made invulnerable by bathing in the dragon's blood.

II

The first known sighting of the Loch Ness monster dates from about 565 A.D. At the lochside of the village of

Abriachan there is a stone from which, legend tells us, the Irish St. Columba, the Abbot of Iona, who brought Christianity to the Picts, would baptize the fierce Highlanders. On this occasion, however, when he was journeying to see the king of the Northern Picts, he found the clansmen burying a man who had been attacked by a water monster. Laying his staff upon the man's chest, he brought him back to life. In another version, one of the Picts, bored by the saint's sermon, swam off across the loch and was killed by the monster. In another version, the man is saved, for as the beast emerges to devour him, St. Columba terrifies the monster with his early Christian voice and commands it to withdraw. Still another legend has it that St. Columba's boat was towed across the loch by one of the monsters; they were granted the everlasting freedom of the loch, as a sign of his gratitude.

Throughout the centuries since St. Columba, there have been numerous sightings of the monster, increasing in frequency with greater accessibility of the Highlands to a larger number of people. The first modern sighting was reported in 1932 by Alex Campbell, water bailiff at Loch Ness. Since that time, investigations have been made on a systematic, scientific basis.

In 1961, the Loch Ness Phenomenon Investigation Bureau was formed. Over a five-month period, it kept five long-range cameras operating continuously, in the event that "Nessie" appeared. Various countries, notably the United States and Japan, sent teams of investigators equipped with sophisticated equipment. To stimulate further investigation, a manufacturer of Scotch whisky offered a reward of one thousand pounds for the capture of the monster. Despite commercialism and high jinks, evidence suggesting the existence of a large unidentified animal continued to accumulate.

A letter from the executive director of the L.N.P.I.B., published in the *Times* of London, Sept. 28, 1970, stated that the organization had acquired several film sequences that "defy ordinary explanation." The Royal Air Force independently examined one roll of film with encouraging results. In addition, Professor Tucker of Birmingham University, England, had made sonar recordings of "large objects behaving in an animate manner" at a depth of several hundred feet.

Despite sonar and photographic evidence, land and loch sightings remain the basis for believing that there might be an unknown animal species in the Loch. However, when the usual standards of evidence are applied, even loosely, the thousands of sightings are reduced to a scant hundred. When such standards are applied with any rigor, there are barely a dozen or so cases which contain all the elements necessary for an ideal sighting. These elements include the names of the observers, date and hour of sighting, the weather and conditions of the Loch, the duration of the observation, the location and distance at which the observation was made (whether from the shore or on the water), and a detailed description of the object.

With repeated sightings, such information should enable us to answer the first of three basic questions: *Are there phenomena occurring in Loch Ness?* The second question is: *Is the object animate?* If the answer to this question is yes, then the description should include the size and shape of its body, the color and texture of its skin, details regarding tail, neck, and head, appendages, if any, and the nature of its movements. Even with all this information, we are still not in a position to answer our third question: *If there are aquatic animals in the Loch, what is the nature of these animals?*

Mere sightings cannot supply us with the answer to that question; for that answer, a prolonged study of their behavior would be necessary. Nevertheless, even with bias on the part of witnesses and the great difficulty in estimating motion, particularly the speed of a moving object, sightings still remain basic to a study of the Loch Ness phenomena.

The water bailiff, Alex Campbell, with over a half century's experience of Loch Ness, had six sightings over the years. One sighting convinced him that there were at least three creatures in the loch, for the humps lay astern of each other, "too far apart to be parts of the same creature." On another occasion he saw the hump of the creature at only five yards' range, and he described its skin as resembling that of an elephant.

During his best sighting, Campbell had stood, at around nine-thirty on a calm May morning, by the mouth of the River Oich, in Fort Augustus, looking across the loch toward Borlum Bay. Suddenly, "a strange object seemed to shoot out of the calm waters almost opposite the Abbey boathouse." When it came to rest, he was able to identify it as a large animal of a type he had never seen before. The neck was about one foot thick; the head, about six feet out of the water, was like a cow's, but flatter. The body was a thirty-foot-long hump.

The animal remained surfaced, restlessly turning its head, until two small boats appeared at the mouth of the Caledonian Canal, at which point it dived, leaving a large turbulence in the water.

At this southernmost point of the loch, where most sightings have occurred, the lake waters flow into the canal past the small village of Fort Augustus and St. Benedict's Abbey. It was there that Brother Richard Horan had a close view of the object in May 1934. Brother Horan was working in the pumphouse near the shore when he heard a noise. At first he ignored it, supposing it to be a boat passing through the entrance to the Caledonian Canal. However, when he looked up, in the words of the investigator's report, he saw an animal:

. . . swimming only 30 yards away from him, parallel with the shore and its head turned toward him. Apparently it had no ears at all, its muzzle was rather blunt, approaching that of a seal—but it was not a seal. It had a graceful neck of 3½ feet in length, held at an angle of 45 degrees to the water with a broad white stripe down the front.

It moved about, changing direction from time to time. Slowly turning toward the S.W., it found a rowing boat in its path. It stopped for a fraction of a minute, causing great commotion in the water. From this point, until it sank, there was a curious motion in the water behind the animal, as if a propeller were working; during this period the animal was lower in the water than before. Finally it dived with a real plunge causing a terrific upheaval (*not* merely sinking).

After its disappearance, the track, resembling that of a torpedo, continued in a N.E. direction.

A similar description was provided to an investigator (Mrs. Constance Whyte)- by Mrs. Finlay and her son Harry, aged twelve. They were vacationing in a trailer parked near the loch. Mr. Finlay had gone into town, and they were peeling potatoes for lunch on the landside of the trailer. Upon hearing a splash, they went around to the lochside to investigate. They found a large, repulsive, reptilian animal along the shoreline.

Mrs. Finley was so fascinated by the head that she scarcely noticed the rest of the animal, except to say that it was about fifteen feet in length and had two or three humps. The head was held erect, and, together with the neck, was about two and a half feet in length. The head alone was about six inches long, about the same width as the neck. There were two six-inch-long projections on the head with a "blob" on each of them. The skin looked black and shiny and it reminded her more of a snail than anything else.

F.W. Holiday later interviewed Mrs. Finlay, as well as a local farmer, Alastair Grant, who also had experienced a remarkable sighting. His occurred about 7:30 on an August evening in 1963, in the company of four other people. It was a hazy night, very calm. The object propelled itself through the water cutting a bow wave and leaving no backwash. There were at least four humps and the object was thirty to forty feet in length. All five observers saw the object about a hundred yards from shore, traveling parallel to them. It was swanlike and had a flat head. When they set out in pursuit, the boat's engine seemed to cause it to submerge, but not before they estimated the length of the neck to be three or four feet. It was definitely black, and they had it under observation for twenty to twenty-five minutes.

Although numerous sightings, apart from those of scientific expeditions, have been made, notably those of F.W. Halliday (June 1965), Peter Davies (August 6, 1967),

John Cameron (May 17, 1967), and Richard Jenkyns (November 10, 1973), they are not substantially different from the early reportings. Discrepancies and similarities appear to be constants. Before turning to the scientific evidence, let us consider briefly those sightings in which Nessie has allegedly been seen on land and consider how much they add to other partial descriptions.

The most famous land sightings have been those of Mr. and Mrs. George Spicer (July 22, 1933) and Arthur Grant (January 5, 1934). The Spicers were driving along the loch when a trunklike object emerged from the bracken on the hillside above the road, about 200 yards ahead of them. The head was two or three feet off the road and undulating its enormous body into two or three arches as it moved. It was at least twenty feet long and elephantine in color. The body, at its fullest, was about five feet in height. It disappeared into the loch, about twenty feet from the road.

Grant, a veterinary student, was motorcycling about one o'clock in the morning from Inverness to his home. The overcast sky along the Loch had cleared and the road was bright with moonlight. About forty yards ahead of him, he noticed a dark object in the bushes on the other side of the road:

"I was almost on it when it turned what I thought was a head on a long neck in my direction. The creature apparently took fright and made two great bounds across the road and then went faster down to the loch, which it entered with a great splash.

"I jumped off my cycle and followed it but from the disturbance on the surface it had evidently made away before I reached the shore. I had a splendid view of the object. In fact I almost struck it with my motorcycle. The body was very hefty. I distinctly saw two front flippers and there seemed to be two other flippers which were behind and which it used to spring from.

"The tail would have been five to six feet long and very powerful; the curious thing about it was that the end was rounded off—it did not come to a point. The total length of the animal would be fifteen to twenty feet."

Later, Grant recalled more details of the animal's appearance, but they are probably less trustworthy than his first impression:

"A head rather like a snake or eel, flat on top, the large oval eye, longish neck and somewhat longer tail. The body much thicker toward the tail than the front portion. In color it was black or dark brown and had a skin rather like a whale. The head must have been about six feet from the ground as it crossed the road, the neck three and a half to four feet long and the tail five or six feet long. Height from belly to back would be about four and a half feet and overall length eighteen to twenty feet."

Many of the witnesses to Nessie have made crude drawings of the animal, but these are little more than footnotes to the photographic evidence we have available. Of all the photographs, the most famous is probably the least reliable. The photographer, Frank Searle, claims to have taken pictures on several occasions, most notably in the early evening of October 21, 1972. In these three shots, the object was lying upon the water's surface with its mouth open. The shape had two humps (the smaller was alleged to be the head), but in all three photos, the shape of the purported animal does not change. Nicholas Witchell, in *The Loch Ness Story*, is of the opinion that the shape of the object's head is "not unlike that of a floating oil drum." He also states that the photos have been tampered with, and that the same photos have been used in another series. In this series, a second hump has been added by means of superimposure or rephotography.

Apart from suspicious content and possible tampering with the print or negative, there remains still a third source for doubt with respect to many Loch Ness photos: inconsistencies of fact regarding the taking of the photo. Unfortunately, some of these elements of doubt exist with regard to the most widely accepted of the Nessie photos, that taken by R. Kenneth Wilson, a London surgeon, on April 1, 1934. Taken in the early morning at a distance of 200 to 300 yards, the first and most famous shot shows a graceful and serpentine neck with a small head in silhouette and below it the wash and counterwash of the ripples its movement caused. Investigator Tim Dinsdale interprets the second, smaller ring of ripples, fourteen feet to the rear, as caused by another part, possibly the tail, of the animal's body.

Maurice Burton, in *The Elusive Monster*, rejects this interpretation, pointing out that there are more concentric circles extending from the left-hand side of the original 8-by-10 print. These did not appear in the original publication in the *Daily Mail* (April 21, 1934). Burton believes the object to be the tail of a diving otter. Roy Mackal, in *The Monster of Loch Ness*, accepts Burton's evaluation but rejects his conclusion, believing the object to be a diving waterfowl, a loon, grebe, cormorant, heron, gull, or possibly a half-wild duck or goose. No critic of the photo has ever maintained that the object shown was not animate.

Such controversies have dogged other well-known photos, by P.A. MacNab, Hugh Gray, and Lachlin Stuart. On the other hand, although not as famous as these surface photos, underwater shots taken by Dr. Robert Rines and his team from the Academy of Applied Science may be conclusive. The first and clearer set was taken on August 8, 1972, the second set on June 20, 1975.

The academy team set up underwater strobe cameras which were triggered by sonar contact with any large moving object, flashing a shot every fifty-five seconds for as long as the object was within sonar range. The range was very short, owing to peat silt, which blackens the water, and did not exceed twenty-five feet.

Estimates of size can be made underwater by comparison with pictures of known objects under the same condition at the known range. The range during the 1972 expedition was fifteen feet. Since objects within a foot or so photographed darkly, and those within a few feet brightly, the animal in these photos was probably five to fifteen feet from the camera. Estimates regarding the size of the "flipper" range from six to eight feet long and two to four feet wide. They are far too large to be appendages of any known aquatic animal in the loch and, indeed, in structure appear to be different from that of any known animal.

The 1975 set of photos were more startling but they were also much vaguer because the cameras were set at a forty-five-foot depth, rather than the earlier thirty-five feet. (The black peat silt thickens rapidly at that level.) The animal was moving almost toward the camera and its skin appeared rough and reddish-brown in color. The head seemed to be a continuation of the neck, as earlier eyewitnesses had described it to be, and the neck was estimated to be about seven feet long. However, a close-up detail of the head was observed at a range of about eight feet, and it was, as Rines properly described it, like the head of a "gargoyle."

The pictures obtained in the 1975 expedition were all taken at different times. An underbelly shot was made at about nine o'clock in the morning, a full body shot at noon, and the head shot in the afternoon. Assuming that it was the same creature in all three shots—a rather large assumption—these time intervals are potentially significant. They might indicate a periodic return on the creature's part, possibly attracted by the flashing of the strobe light because its curiosity was aroused. It may, on the other hand, have been following some feeding pattern of its own.

Today, the investigative process is carried on more through motion-picture than still photography. Motion pictures introduced an entirely new dimension into the identification of the creature. In addition to providing a more complete physiological description because the object(s) is under observation for a greater length of time, there is yet another advantage. Films permit us to study the animal's movements, thus learning something of its behavior. From its behavior alone, it is possible to identify an animal and sometimes to determine something of its biological makeup which is not available readily to observation with the naked eye. For example, from speeds attained by the animal in the film, we may deduce the presence of a long and powerful tail. Further, from its submergence patterns we may reasonably conclude whether or not the animal possesses a hydrostatic mechanism.

The possibility of hoaxes and frauds is considerably less than with still photography, at least with regard to internal evidence. While external evidence or circumstances of the filming and the availability of the films are suspect in some cases, the content of a film is much more difficult to fake than in still photography. A film, of course, is composed of many individual stills which follow one another rapidly during projection, thus giving the impression of continuity. The position of the object differs in one still only minutely from its position in the previous and following one. Any attempt to fake one still necessitates faking the one before and after it, until at last the entire sequence must be faked. Whereas a single photo may be fraudulent and go undetected, it is almost impossible to fake an entire sequence of stills in close sequence without detection. Any cutting or other editing would, of course, immediately make the film suspect.

The strongest evidence is offered by the films of Malcom Irvine (1934), James Fraser (1934), and G.E. Taylor (1938), and the most famous film of the Loch Ness monster, that of Tim Dinsdale, taken on April 23, 1960, at Foyers, at a distance of 1,300 yards. It shows an object which cannot be identified. Lasting about five minutes, the film was made with a 16mm Rolex movie camera on black-and-white film. It used a telescopic lens from an elevation of about 300 feet. Later from the same position, filming a boat whose size and speed were known provided the needed calibrations to estimate the length of the object at fifteen feet and the speed at 7 to 10 mph.

Examining the object through 7X binoculars, Dinsdale described the object as mahogany in color, "with a back like an underfed horse," a description which had been used by previous witnesses. On its left flank there was a dark spot, like the dapple of a cow. At first it was motionless in the water, a long, oval shape with no sign of a dorsal fin. Abruptly, it began to move, obtaining speeds estimated by JARIC (the Royal Air Force's Joint Air Reconnaissance Intelligence Center) to be faster than those of the boat which Dinsdale photographed.

In January 1966, the air force unit enlarged and examined every frame of the Dinsdale film. They estimated the length of the boat to be 13.5 feet, with a speed of 6.5 mph. The actual length of the boat was 15 feet and it was moving at 7 mph. Their accuracy with regard to the boat makes their other estimates of Dinsdale's film worthy of serious attention.

The team of air force experts concluded that the object was 3 to 3.7 feet out of the water and at least 5.5 feet in length. They also said that the original hump was between 12 and 16 feet in length and that the object could not possibly have been a surface craft. "Even if the object is relatively flat-bellied, the normal body 'rounding' in nature would suggest that there is at least two feet under the water from which it may be deduced that a cross section through the object would be *not less* than six feet wide and five feet high." But more important, the Royal Air Force investigators concluded that "it probably is an animate object."

We have probably learned all that we are apt to learn from still and motion-picture photography with cameras operating at a surface level. Beyond verification of an existing creature, there seems to be little more that such methods can teach us. Of course, it is always possible that clearer shots of the animal's entire body may be taken, but given that we appear to be dealing with a creature that inhabits deep water and rarely surfaces, it is unlikely. Future expeditions will doubtless concern themselves increasingly with underwater explorations, using photography as an adjunct to sonar probes.

Sonic investigation of Loch Ness did not really get under way until the preliminary expedition of Dr. Peter F. Baker in 1960 and the Cambridge-Oxford expedition of 1962. The most successful of the later expeditions have been those of Prof. D.G. Tucker and Dr. Hugh Braithwaite (1968), and more recently those of Robert Love (1969), Dr. Robert H. Rines (1970), Prof. Roy Mackal (1970), and the New York *Times*–sponsored expedition of 1976, led by Rines.

The evidence obtained from these sonar experiments has achieved scientific validity and has met basic scientific criteria; primarily, the appearance of large moving objects in the depths of the loch have been shown to be (1) multiple, and (2) capable of reproducible corroboration. Further, these phenomena have been localized along the bottom and the sides of the loch and occasionally toward the center of the waterway. The general depth at which contact is made and the movement patterns suggest non-air-breathing animals. These objects appear both singly and in small groups. They attain horizontal speeds up to 17 mph and depth changes up to 5 mph; this rules out the possibility of their being large fish with closed swim bladders. They are asymmetrical and elongated in shape and attain a size of approximately twenty feet. A few sonar contacts suggest, but do not confirm, that they may have sinusoidal flexure (projections) or periodic physical features (humps).

III

Certainly, the evidence in favor of Loch Ness phenomena, whether animate or inanimate, whether of a prehistoric or existing animal, will doubtless continue to mount. So, at this point in our investigation of the mystery of the loch, let us sum up the evidence and consider exactly what we have really found out.

FREQUENCY OF APPEARANCE—BY YEAR

The peak years for sightings have been 1933–1934, 1960, and 1964–1969. However, there is not much which can be deduced from these statistics, since the animal's appearances are correlated with human behavior. With more workmen, tourists, and scientists around the loch, more sightings would be the expected result.

FREQUENCY OF APPEARANCE— BY MONTH

The peak months are July and August, but again, this statistic probably reflects human behavior rather than that of the "monster." However, there is the possibility the animals hibernate during the winter months, and some correlation might be made between the months of its appearance and the waxing and waning of the food supply, but this correlation seems quite tenuous.

FREQUENCY OF APPEARANCE—
BY TIME OF DAY

In 1959, Tim Dinsdale distributed the frequency of appearances according to the hour at which the sightings were made. He determined that 85 percent of the major sightings were made between dawn and nine-thirty in the morning. However, in 1976 Roy Mackal performed the same plotting of sightings and arrived at quite different results; his results indicate that most appearances occur late in the afternoon.

It is possible, however, that these statistics may be accounted for by the greater number of people about in the early morning and later in the day, passing to and from their jobs. The sudden drop in sightings during the lunch hour might be taken to confirm this view.

FREQUENCY OF APPEARANCE—
BY LOCATION

Unfortunately, these efforts to establish a frequency distribution have not been more successful than the foregoing ones. Sightings have most often taken place at the south end of the loch (near Fort Augustus), at the northern end (near Abriachan and Dores), off the north shore (near Drumnadrochit and Achnahannet) and off the south shore (near Foyers). In a word, opposite the most heavily populated areas of the loch.

DURATION

Most sightings last only a few minutes. This is important because the suggestions have been made that when it surfaces, the animal is basking or that it is in search of food. Its surfacings are far too brief, and this fact tells us something of what the animal's behavior is not, and therefore tells us what it could *not* be.

BODY SIZE

Most estimates range from fifteen or twenty feet to a maximum of fifty feet. According to the analysis of the LNIB, 39.65 percent of all sightings report a body length, exclusive of head and tail, of eleven to twenty-five feet, with the greatest single figure of 18.39 percent placing the torso at eleven to fifteen feet. Professor Mackal estimates that a large, twenty-foot "monster" would be about four feet in diameter, or twelve and a half feet in circumference.

BODY SHAPE

"Humps" are reported in 45 percent of the sightings. Dinsdale estimates the humps average about five to six feet in length and three to four feet above water level. The humps have been seen to change in size and number and shape. This fact has led some experts to suggest that the humps are vertical undulations which might be used to propel the animal. Others suggest that the humps are bodily structures, not related, however, directly to the backbone. Still another theory, which explains the variation and attempts to explain the submergence pattern of the animal, is the inflatable-air-sac theory. When fully inflated, the air sac causes the back to appear as one hump, and when deflated, usually as two or three humps. Acting as ballast, it permits the animal to sink vertically, rather than in the usual manner of diving.

HEAD AND NECK

The head and neck are of about the same diameter, giving this part of the body an eellike or reptilian appearance, with the head barely distinguishable. Both head and neck are about five to six feet in length, tapering somewhat, with a diameter of about one foot.

FEATURES

Hornlike antennae have been mentioned in some reports, but they probably should not be taken for ears. Aquatic life does not normally have ears because it has no need of them. The mouth is some twelve to eighteen inches in width.

TAIL

The tail may be laterally flattened, as Mackal suggests,

but more reliable is the consensus that the tail is about six feet long and presumably used in swimming. Overall the average length of the animals reported in Loch Ness would be between twenty-two and twenty-seven feet.

COLOR

The animal is consistently described as blackish brown, black, sometimes with a greenish tint, to elephant or battleship gray, to reddish brown, tending toward a lighter, almost yellowish brown, especially on the underside of the animal. Colors, especially dark ones, are always darkened by distance because less of the light reflected from them is seen by the eye. The conclusion, then, that the animals are brown is supported by a recent color photo taken by Robert Rines. Variations in the shadings of brown may be attributed to age or sex or simply to the fact that different animals were being viewed.

SPEED

Eyewitnesses are easily mistaken with regard to motion. Fortunately, sonar trackings are reliable and indicate that there are three types of speed: "bursts" of 15-17 mph, cruising speeds of about 10 mph, and diving speeds up to 5 mph.

MOVEMENT

One of the commonly described patterns of movement is that of an object at rest or gliding which suddenly takes off with a great burst of speed and then submerges. This pattern suggests an animal waiting for its prey. Another common pattern is the zigzag, which suggests the animal is hesitant or searching for its food.

LOCOMOTION

The speeds attained would not be reached merely by the use of one or two appendages, such as flippers; therefore, the major means of locomotion must be by the lateral movement of its tail. The appendages would appear to be used primarily for a change of direction.

TURBULENCE

Both the words "wake" and "wash" seem to be used interchangeably to describe the turbulence which is noticed near the object, but which may or may not be connected with its movement. Even when due allowance has been made, the V-shaped wake is probably caused by the movement of the animal's body, and the wash by the propulsion of its tail.

SURFACING

From the rarity of sightings, it would appear that the creatures surface at night primarily, or rarely break the surface when breathing, or are non-air breathers who surface for other reasons. Surfacing patterns have no meaning for the night surfacers and non-air breathers, since in neither case is there any likely connection between surfacing and respiration. The rarity of sightings makes the food supply also an unlikely explanation.

Sirenian mammals normally do not surface, however, but only put their nostrils above the water in order to breathe. This feature would account for the rarity of sightings.

SUBMERGENCE

Opposed to the traditional diving of water birds and such, the submergence pattern appears to be one of sinking straight down. The normal diving pattern may be employed only when the animal is frightened. However, the head and tail are difficult to distinguish and a diving motion might also be difficult to detect.

The vertical sinking pattern has been observed by sonar readings at great depth. This fact would appear to indicate that the creatures have lungs which operate as a hydraulic system, similar to the open swim bladders in many fish. They may also be able to pump water in and out of their lungs. But whatever the diving mechanism of the "monster" may ultimately prove to be, there is no biological reason why the rapid depth changes of the Loch Ness creature cannot occur.

SOUND

Nessie's sensitivity to sound—sudden shouts from tourists, the motors of passing boats, the sudden slamming of car doors by excited vacationers—has been frequently reported. Hearing does not require the development of an outward ear, but only of an inner one. Sirenian mammals and certain reptiles are extremely sensitive to sound. Many forms of aquatic life do not depend on airborne sound waves, but respond to underwater sound waves by receiving vibrations through some portion of their bodies.

The whole question of how the Loch Ness creature hears bears importantly on the question of whether it uses sonic waves in order to "see" in the black waters of the loch and whether it is able to communicate.

COMMUNICATION

Random sounds—the roars, barks, hissings, clickings, thuds, and squeaks of the animal kingdom—are not true communication, although doubtless they possess meaning. The meaning is equivalent to a human's cry of pain, anger, or surprise. True communication requires a pattern of repeated sounds, such as are made by dolphins and whales. The underwater sounds of Nessie do not appear capable of such sophistication, but as the hydrophonic experiments of Mackal, Edgerton, and others in 1970 proved, the creature has a repertoire of varied, animate sounds.

REPRODUCTION

Unless we are going to presume the entrapment of a single creature in the Loch and grant it a longevity unknown to any other species, we must presume some manner of reproduction. We must assume that they do not change their environment to spawn, hatch eggs, or give live birth on shore. We must, therefore, assume they reproduce in the water.

As we have seen, much of the present data is incomplete and requires more than the usual amount of interpretation; the problem is to remain completely objective without excluding our powers of intuition. Nevertheless, on the basis of the present state of research, certain facts appear to be firmly established and a few tentative conclusions are possible. It does, indeed, appear evident that some form of animate life exists, but what is it?

It is very possible that the Loch Ness creatures are descendants of a prehistoric species or some mutation thereof. Most of the evidence, especially the underwater photographs of Dr. Rines, would tend to suggest the pleiosaur, but this animal was a reptile and could not live in the cold waters of the Loch and, in addition, does not appear to have been able to breathe underwater.

Only slightly less probable is that they may be a previously unknown animal. This possibility is not as unlikely as it may at first appear. Very little is known about creatures in the depths of the ocean, and it might prove that Nessie is related to one of these. Some form of mutation would be necessary, however, since the water pressure at the ocean's depth and those of Loch Ness are vastly different.

A third possibility is that they may be a mutation of some presently known species. Biologists, of course, would prefer the excitement of discovering a new species, but it is more probable that Nessie is a giant mutation of some known, existing species.

The author's own view, as I have expressed before, is that the creature is a mutation of the giant eel, but the reader now has the facts before him and may very reasonably take a different view.

IV

Whether the mystery of Loch Ness is ever resolved to everyone's satisfaction or not, the dragon or the sea serpent will still be with us, according to some modern psychologists. One such expert, C.G. Jung, writes that the sea serpent represents "the negative mother-imago, thus expressing resistance to incest, or the fear of it." The dragon's guardianship of treasure represents, according to the same author, the mother's apparent possession of the son's libido; in psychological terms, the treasure which is hard to attain lies hidden in the unconscious.

Elsewhere, in his *Man and His Symbols*, Jung writes: "The familiar myth of Jonah and the whale, or the hero swallowed by a sea serpent which enchains him to the sea, night, the west, symbolizes the supposed course of the sun from evening to dawn, according to J.L. Henderson. He is ensconced in darkness which represents a kind of death. . . . The struggle between the heroes and the dragon . . . appears to allow . . . the perpetual theme of the triumph of self over regressive tendencies. The majority of people remain unconscious of the dark negative side of their personalities. Heroes, on the contrary, must make an accounting of the shadows which exist and from which they draw their power. It is necessary that man reach an accord with his destructive powers if he is going to become strong enough to conquer the dragon. In other words, the self cannot triumph until it has mastered and assimilated darkness."

While Jung's theory can neither be proved or disproved, the enduring fascination of Nessie will probably survive our scientific efforts to unmask her. Her myth strikes a chord somewhere deep in our psyches. Even though we say today that we no longer believe in monsters, and never did believe in Nessie, we will probably go on attaching to them the same meanings out ancestors did . . . even if we only "believe" in them in our dreams.

The Devil's Hoofprints

Eric J. Dingwall

No known animal, and certainly no human, could have left these imprints in the sands. They were reminiscent of similar prints, equally unexplained, that have been found in the United States. And now, here in England, they had once again been observed. Did the devil walk again? Dr. Eric J. Dingwall, one of the most distinguished but also one of the most skeptical of twentieth-century psychic researchers, asks: What kind of creature could scale a cliff, walk into the sea, pass through fences, and leave tracks on roof tops and walls?

Of all the strange stories to which I have listened for so many years, that told by Mr. Wilson was one of the oddest and the most inexplicable. Indeed, Mr. Wilson himself was so completely bewildered by his extraordinary experience that he had only confided it to three highly trusted friends, a canon of the Church, a doctor, and a customs officer. The thing was impossible. It could not have happened. And yet Mr. Wilson knew that it had happened and that it had happened to him.

One day when Mr. Wilson was merely reading his newspaper by a fire, his heart began to beat more quickly. So he had not been the only one! Others had had the same strange experience and could no more explain it than he could. Now at least people could not say that he was lying, mad, or suffering from delusions.

So it happened that he wrote off to me, since my name was mentioned in the article he had read, and in careful, soberly phrased terms he told me his story. I confess that my own interest in it almost exceeded his own, and so at the first opportunity I hastened down to the little village where Mr. Wilson carries on his business.

I found him in a little office. He was a tall, well-built man with a kindly smile and an assured manner, obviously no imaginative dreamer of tall stories.

When we had made ourselves comfortable Mr. Wilson began to tell me something about himself and his history. He had not always lived in a village, where he had now built up for himself a neat little business. Years before he had been the proprietor of a flourishing concern in New York, but after the Wall Street crash he had lost a good deal of money and decided to return to England. At first he found himself working for others but, being a man of sturdy independence, he finally set up on his own. And it was when taking a short holiday at a West Coast watering place where he had spent his childhood that *it* happened.

It was in 1950, Mr. Wilson said, that he went down to the West Country to stay in the Devonshire coast town where he had spent so many happy days of his youth. Never could he forget that holiday as long as he lived, for it was on the last day of his stay that it happened. On that day he decided on impulse to go and look at his old home and walk again on the beach where he had played in his childhood years. This little beach is entirely enclosed by rocks and steep cliffs and is invisible from above. The only entrance is by a passage through the cliffs which is closed by a tall iron gate. This gate is used as a pay gate in summer and is locked up in winter. On that October afternoon the gate was locked, but Mr. Wilson's old home was almost opposite the gate and he remembered that it was possible to get around the gate by going through the garden of the house. So he did this, and was soon on the sands of the beach, which was deserted and gloomy on that autumn day. The sea had been to the top of the beach but now the tide had gone out, leaving the sand as smooth as glass. Mr. Wilson looked at the sand and could hardly believe his eyes. For starting at the top of the beach and just below the perpendicular cliff was a clear single line of marks, apparently hoofmarks of some biped, which were clearly impressed upon the wet sand almost as if cut out with some sharp instrument. The marks were about six feet apart and ran from the cliff in a straight line down the center of the narrow beach and into the sea.

Mr. Wilson's first reaction seems to have been intense curiosity. He approached the prints and examined them with the most careful attention. He tried to jump from one mark to another and then, removing his shoes and socks, tried to see if he could match them with his own stride. But they were so far apart that he could not reach from one to the next, although he was a tall man with long legs. The hoofmarks, which were not cloven, resembled those which might have been made by a large unshod pony, and the impressions were deeper than those which he himself made with his shoes on, even though he weighed some sixteen stone. What he particularly noticed at the time was that no sand was splashed up at the edges: it looked as if each mark had been cut out of the sand with a flat iron.

After Mr. Wilson had told me his story and had seen that I treated it seriously, and showed no inclination to disbelieve him, he went on to tell me how, after examining the footprints, he had realized how inexplicable they were. For here was a biped with a track shaped like a hoof, starting immediately beneath a perpendicular cliff on a closed beach and ending in the sea. There was no returning track. I asked if it were possible that the animal, or whatever it might have been, could have turned to right or left in the sea and regained the land at some other point. But Mr. Wilson produced photographs which showed that the beach was a comparatively narrow space completely enclosed by rocky headlands on either side. What possible creature, from land or water, could have made such footprints as these? And what size could it have been to have so long a stride? What kind of hoof would make so clear-cut an impression? As Mr. Wilson said, what might he have seen if he had arrived a little earlier, for the receding tide was only just beyond the last print of the line? After asking himself questions such as these, Mr. Wilson wondered if perhaps there was something uncanny about the footprints. For were it a sea animal why should it be provided with hard hoofs? If it were a land animal why should it walk into the sea, and where did it go when it got there? Or did it have wings? In any case, what known animal could make such a track?

Questions very like these had been asked before, and it was just because Mr. Wilson had accidentally come across a reference to another case of mysterious tracks that he had written to me. For just over a hundred years ago—in 1855 to be precise—there had been a night of heavy snowfall in the neighborhood of Exeter and southward into Devon, and when the countryfolk awoke, a strange sight met their eyes. For there upon the snow were odd foot tracks resembling hoofmarks, which seemed to be those of a biped rather than those of any four-footed creature. Each mark was about eight inches ahead of the next and the prints were so widely distributed over a large area that it seemed that more than one creature must have been involved. But what was still more mysterious was the route taken by this animal. The prints were not only on the ground but also on the roofs of houses, on the tops of walls, and even on enclosed areas like courtyards.

The prints caused the utmost concern and consternation and discussion about them raged in the press for several weeks. Every kind of animal was suggested and then rejected. Some thought that the tracks were made by badgers or by birds; others thought that an escaped kangaroo was responsible, or possibly a racoon. Gradually the excitement died down and the villagers were no longer frightened to come out of their cottages for fear that Satan himself would again be walking. And so the devil's hoofmarks remained an unsolved mystery.

It was not till 1908 that the strange footprints were seen again, this time in the United States, from Newark to Cape May in New Jersey. Here again were reports of marks like the hoofs of a pony in the thick snow, and again we have the story of how the tracks led up to wire fences and then continued on the other side, even when the uprights were only a few inches apart. No solution seems to have been reached and eventually the New Jersey Devil was forgotten, just like his predecessor in the Devon countryside.

What are we to make of these stories and what was it that made the strange prints that so astonished Mr. Wilson on that October afternoon? The more questions one asks, the more baffling does the case become. There may be a simple explanation for this experience, just as there may be for the two or three previous cases reported, of which Mr. Wilson knew nothing. So far no one has thought of one. If anyone does, no one will be more happy than my friend Mr. Wilson, and those who hear his story will not be tempted to think that, on a Devon beach in 1950, he had all but seen the devil walking again.

King Tut's Curse

Gordon Thistlewaite

*The twentieth century rediscovered one of ancient
Egypt's most colorful, mysterious, and dramatic pharaohs,
the boy king Tutankhamen. The gold and other artifacts
from King Tut's burial chambers made the rounds of the
world's great museums, and millions gazed at the skill and
wealth of a world long dead. Mr. Thistlewaite examines
another aspect of public fascination: the curse of Tutankhamen which seems to have clung to the king's tomb since
it was excavated by European archaeologists, and appears to have found expression in a series of deaths that
have befallen those associated with the pharaoh's tomb.*

In Cairo, Egypt, on Monday, December 19, 1966, a car
struck down Mohammed Ibrahim, fracturing his skull and
inflicting other injuries that caused his death two days
later. Mr. Ibrahim, the Egyptian government's Director of
Antiquities, was struck as he left a conference with French
diplomats at the Ministry of Culture.

For four months Ibrahim had fought against Egypt's
decision to send relics from the famous "cursed tomb" of
Pharaoh Tutankhamen to an exhibition in Paris. When he
finally concurred, his daughter was seriously injured in an
auto smash-up. He began to have dreams that he was to

die. Unnerved, he made an appointment with the Minister of Culture to seek reconsideration of the government's agreement. French representatives attended the meeting.

At the conference, Ibrahim was finally prevailed upon to withdraw his objection. It was pointed out that the government had, some months before, officially pronounced the curse to be only a superstition and out of keeping with socialist philosophy. However, as Mohammed Ibrahim left the meeting, superstition turned into reality as death bore down upon him with the swift wings of steel and iron.

The eighteen-year-old Pharaoh Tutankhamen had been buried with a splendor unmatched in Egypt both before and after his time. His tomb, uncovered thirty-three centuries later, was said to have had a curse attached to it. That rumor, which circulated even before the tomb was entered, gained credence with the extraordinary death of George E. S. M. Herbert, fifth Earl of Carnarvon, who had financed and collaborated with archaeologist Howard Carter in searching for the tomb. Deaths occurred with disturbing frequency among those who had had anything to do with the opening of the burial place in the bleak and arid Biban-el-Maluk, the Valley of the Kings. A full listing would be impossible here, but the following may give an idea of why a sense of awe and uneasiness spread rapidly around the world.

Sir Archibald Douglas-Reid, the radiologist appointed to X-ray the mummy, died on his way to the tomb. Frank Raleigh, a photographer, went blind and died. Egyptologist H. E. Evelyn-White wrote a letter saying he knew there was a curse on him and committed suicide. Howard Carter's secretary died. He had taken from the tomb an alabaster vase which bore the inscription, "Death shall come on swift wings to him that toucheth the tomb of Pharaoh."

His father, Lord Westbury, inherited the vase. According to a dispatch from Universal News Service in February, 1930: "Lord Westbury was frequently heard to mutter, 'the curse of the pharaoh,' as though this preyed on his mind. In his last letter he wrote, 'I cannot stand this horror any more and am going to make an exit.'" Westbury threw himself from the window of his suite in London, plunging through a glass canopy on his way to instant death on the sidewalk. His funeral hearse struck and killed eight-year-old Joseph Greer on its way to the graveyard.

Many more deaths occurred among those who had visited the tomb. And yet, many who might have been expected to die lived on to their normal life expectancy or beyond and then died of natural causes. Among these was Howard Carter, who actually opened the tomb and died at the age of sixty-seven in 1939. Professor James Breasted of the University of Chicago said, "I defy the curse and if anyone was exposed to it, I was. I slept in that tomb for two weeks. I even had my meals there." Breasted lived to the age of seventy and died in 1935. Sir Flinders Petrie, the father of Egyptology, died at eighty-nine; Professor P. E. Newberry died at eighty; Sir Edward A. Wallis Budge died at seventy-seven. All had been prominent in examining the tomb and all died from natural causes.

At first glance, it would appear that one can find plenty of support for the belief in a curse on Tutankhamen's tomb and that, conversely, one can find just as much support for the idea's being only a superstition. But, as we are going to see, this does not allow for the modern occultist's understanding of how a curse works.

The only written curse on Tutankhamen's tomb was that inscribed on the alabaster vase that Lord Westbury inherited from his dead son. There is an apocryphal story that when Carnarvon found the vase, he put his hand inside it, drawing it out to discover blood on one of his fingers. This in itself could have launched the rumor of a curse, but the fact is that the existence of a curse was known well before that incident.

From the occult standpoint, a curse need not be written out; but, if it is reduced to writing and thus made known to the accursed, it becomes that much more effective. In fact, once known to the accursed individual, the curse may work through normal psychological means without reference to any occult force. Very frequently, though by no means always, Egyptian tombs were cursed. This we know not only from the literature of the times, but also from inscribed curses found on some of the tombs.

From literature, for example, we know some methods of

imposing a curse. Powerful slaves, dedicated to the pharaoh, were slowly tortured until they were all but out of their minds. At the same time injunctions were read to them that they must continue to guard the pharaoh in the next life as they had in this. When they had been brainwashed with that idea, they were instantly killed. The feeling was that their anguished, single-minded spirits would make the most hostile tomb guardians. Of course, we can have no idea of how many tombs were cursed in this way. Perhaps more than we would like to believe.

Some curses did carry elaborate inscriptions. One on the mummy of Pharaoh Seti I began: "The cobras on my crown will spew flames of fire on him who distrubs my rest. . . ." There was another: "As for anyone who enters this tomb, my spirit will pounce upon him as on a bird and he shall be judged by the great god. . . ." And yet another: "The Sun god shall punish him who injures my tomb or drags out my mummy. . . ." Such inscriptions pale beside the malefic sophistication of the torture method, however, and this has always suggested to me that they were intended only to scare away the professional tomb robbers. In this they were not too successful for, according to the Abbot Papyrus, in the reign of Ramses IX, about 200 years after Tutankhamen, it was necessary to wage an all-out police campaign against the thieves.

But there is very good reason to believe that Tutankhamen's tomb was cursed and cursed with the most furious malediction possible. We'll find there was good reason for this, along with the mystery of why a do-nothing king whose only distinction, according to Howard Carter, was to die and get buried should have received the most elaborate funeral in Egyptian history.

For sixteen years archaeologist Howard Carter and Lord Carnarvon, his backer, had looked for the tomb of Tutankhamen in the Valley of the Kings. They knew it was buried there because of the evidence of remnants of the funeral observance which bore the king's name. By November 1922, the Carnarvon permit to explore was about to expire. He went to London. Carter, with only four days left, made one more try and found the buried stairway leading to the tomb.

He cabled Carnarvon in London, and the peer, with his daughter Evelyn, went at once to Egypt. They watched as Carter made a hole and peered into the tomb. They had had only a glimpse into an antechamber, but it was filled with furniture of solid gold. And that was only the beginning. Clearing a tomb takes a lot of time. Every tiny detail must be photographed, measured, and catalogued before being moved. While the preliminary work was going on, Carnarvon and his daughter went back to England.

The London *Times* carried the story of the discovery, and it came to the attention of Count Louis Hamon, the famous psychic and palm-reader who went by the name of Cheiro. The very evening he read the story, he was visited by his guide, an Egyptian girl. The girl indicated a writing pad. Cheiro went into a trance and produced through automatic writing a message which read: "Lord Carnarvon must not enter tomb. If he does, he will suffer sickness and death will claim him in Egypt."

Cheiro wrote to Carnarvon at once, but the latter had his own seer, a man named Velma. Velma gave him a reading and summed up his findings, "I see danger for you, probably arising out of your interest in the occult." Carnarvon went away in a somber mood. He was a worried man. Before he left again for Egypt he saw Velma. This time Velma used a crystal ball.

Velma reported seeing an Egyptian scene. He saw a temple, mourners, and an aging priest placing a mask of gold on the head of a mummy. He saw the tomb with Carnarvon near it. Lightning flashes erupted from the tomb and enveloped Carnarvon until he was standing alone in their midst. Velma said, "I see disaster for you. Abandon the work." Carnarvon admitted that he felt a strange influence at work, urging him to give up the project, but he refused to do so. With his daughter, he sailed back to Egypt.

There, before hundreds of spectators and newsmen, Carnarvon and his party prepared to open the tomb's second chamber. As the time arrived, he rose and said jestingly, "All right, everyone. I think we're ready for our little concert in the tomb." And one of the newspapermen said, "If he goes down in that spirit, I give him six weeks to live. . . ."

One day as Carnarvon emerged from the tomb a mosquito bit him on the face. That was unusual because the valley is mosquito-free due to lack of water. The next morning, when Carnarvon was shaving with his straight razor, he nicked the mosquito bite. He dabbed at the spot with cotton and iodine; however, that evening he ran a temperature of 101 and felt a chill. He took to his bed. Some kind of poisoning was apparently at work. He was prostrate for ten days, then developed pneumonia and died. At the moment Carnarvon died, every light in the city went out and stayed out for five minutes. The Cairo Electricity Board found fuses and circuit breakers intact and was never able to assign a reason to the eerie event.

Though the tomb was discovered in 1922, the careful progress of the archaeologists did not result in the opening of the king's coffin until late in 1925. And just as Velma had seen in his crystal ball three years earlier, the face of the mummy was covered by a lifelike mask of gold.

Now we come to the question of why an obscure pharaoh was given the most elaborate funeral in the history of Egypt. And why was so potent a curse apparently laid upon his tomb? The era from which Tutankhamen rose was a historical cesspool, a nightmare of vice and intrigue. It had its beginning nearly fifty years before when Pharaoh Amenophis III married Tiy, a princess of the Mitanni kingdom. The pharaoh's grandfather, Thutmose III, had grouped all priesthoods under the High Priest of Amon and made him great seer of the realm. As such he prophesied on state events. When a boy was born to young Tiy, the prophecy about him was such that his father had him raised in exile, probably at the court of Mitanni. After the child's birth his name never appeared in records until the death of his father, when he then returned to Egypt and assumed the throne. He brought with him the idea of a new religion, which, of course, brought him into conflict with the High Priest of Amon. This, along with hating the priest for the prophecy that exiled him, resulted in the new pharaoh moving his court from Thebes to the north. He called his new capital Akhet-Aton. He dropped the word "Amon" from his name and called himself Akhnaton.

For a long time, history regarded Akhnaton as a heroic humanist, a great religious reformer. He banned all the gods of Egypt and made the state religion the worship of one god—Aton. He patronized poets and painters, and, indeed, some of the artwork of his time, showing chiaroscuro and perspective, was not to be matched again until the Renaissance. . . . In the meantime, he neglected his political responsibilities. His regents in Egypt's various dominions called on him vainly for help, but he was too wrapped up in art, poetry, religion, and his family life. Somewhat of a narcissist, he often had himself and his entire family portrayed in the nude. His wife was the beautiful Nefertiti, whose bust is one of the best-known pieces of sculpture in the world.

For twelve years Akhnaton let the empire crumble while he played with his family. Nefertiti bore him six daughters.

Archaeologists puzzled long over the presence of a seventh daughter who always seemed to be linked to Tiy, Akhnaton's mother, rather than to Nefertiti. They grew uneasy when they found that Tiy wore the double plumes of empire, and even more so when Tiy, not Nefertiti, bore the title of Great Wife. Shock followed when it was discovered that the seventh princess, Beketaten, was Tiy's child by her son Akhnaton. In short, the king's mother was now his wife and the mother of his daughter-sister. Nefertiti had been replaced.

Now two young princes appear upon the scene, Smenkare and Tutankhamen. We do not know for certain who their mothers were, but we can speculate. Scientists agree that they were both fathered by Akhnaton. It is my opinion, based on comparing the features of the princes with those of Tiy and Nefertiti, that Smenkare was Nefertiti's son and Tutankhamen was Tiy's.

Smenkare married Meritaten, one of Nefertiti's daughters. Tutankhamen married Ankhesenpaaton, another daughter, but not before she bore a child to her father. Akhnaton then appointed his son Smenkare co-ruler and, at the same time, appears to have been involved in an unnatural affair with him. At this point, something in the nature of a revolution occurred, though records on it are missing. We know only that Egypt was in dire trouble. There was a vast body of unemployed. The borders of the empire were crumbling and no more riches were flowing into the country. And the king himself was given to vices that were anathema to the Egyptians.

In the kingdom of Mitanni, from which Tiy came and where Akhnaton was raised, it was regarded almost as a religious sacrament for a son to have a child by his mother. The custom was known as *xvetokdas* and was the second of the seven good works of religion. But to the Egyptians, although they recognized second-degree marriages (brother/sister), marriage in the first degree was an unspeakable sin. Akhnaton was deposed. Tiy killed herself—and Nefertiti vanished. None of their mummies has ever been found.

With Tiy's death and Akhnaton (probably) exiled, Smenkare now took over the throne, and Ay, Tiy's brother, became Chamberlain and Great Priest. Ay advised the king to make an expedition to strengthen his dominions and try to win back the border lands. While Smenkare was away (and it seems he never returned), Ay put his nephew, the twelve-year-old Tutankhamen, on the throne, meanwhile plotting and planning the devious way in which he himself could gain total control. And so it happened that after six years the young boy mysteriously died at the age of eighteen, leaving his doe-eyed queen, Ankhesenpaaton, his sole survivor. Ay, by default, became the next pharaoh.

Carefully repeated, over and over again in Tutankhamen's tomb, inscriptions tell how it was Ay who was responsible for the lavish entombment. He seems to have made sure he got the credit. Yet, as Howard Carter pointed out, at no other time in Egyptian history did a pharaoh ever take credit for burying a predecessor. Why then was this so?

Ay was afraid. The ancient Egyptians subscribed to severe ethical beliefs. Before the spirit could pass through the Hall of Truth after death, it had to justify itself. Other souls could rise up against it, as Tutankhamen's could against Ay. But Ay had a way of buying himself off. The goal of the Egyptian was undisturbed rest among all the effects he might possibly need in the hereafter.

So Ay made sure that Tutankhamen would rest forever in the most lavishly equipped tomb in Egypt. He made sure nothing was wanting that might make the pharaoh's sleep restless, even to including a carefully labeled lock of hair from the head of his mother, Tiy. The spirit of the young pharaoh would have no reason to wander abroad in the night, nor would it rise up against Ay at the Judgment, forever barring him from Amenti.

But, as Velma is reported to have told Lord Carnarvon, "Wherever a place has been the focus of tremendous emotion, there is not the slightest doubt that something—I don't know what—persists." Thus, despite whatever powerful curse Ay laid on Tutankhamen's tomb, there was something else to be considered. The affair of Tutankhamen represented the point at which all of the wretched emotions of Akhnaton's court converged, all the incest, vice, depravity, and insanity, despair, and deceit; all the thwarted ambition, the treachery, the homicides, the suicides, the gnawing guilts were symbolized in that lavish entombment, fermenting like some evil wine, sealed in a bottle of gold.

Carnarvon and Carter uncorked that bottle.

We are still left with the problem of why Carnarvon died and not Carter; why Egyptologist Evelyn-White killed himself and Sir Flinders Petrie lived to be eighty-nine; why Carter himself was not affected, but Lord Westbury was driven to death by the mere presence of the vase. We know more today of the mechanics of a curse than we did fifty years ago. Papers on curse pathology appear in orthodox medical journals.

The late Adrian Dobbs, the mathematical genius of Cambridge University, saw a transfer of psychic energy in subatomic particles he named psitrons. Such a particle carries a "bit" of information to a critically poised neuron in a receptive subject, causing that neuron to fire. A chain reaction is set up; other neurons become involved and the subject perceives. The only condition for the interaction is that the first neuron be critically poised when the psitron hits.

We might guess then, if we allow Dobbs's theories, that the maliciously charged psitrons saturating the tomb of Tutankhamen fired poised neurons in receptive nervous systems and passed harmlessly through others. That some profound psychic influence was at work is most directly evidenced by one fact. It was nearly three years after Carnarvon's death that Tutankhamen's mummy was unwrapped and examined by pathologists. They found on the cheek of the mummy a wound exactly like the mosquito bite that had caused Carnarvon's death!

The Treasure of Lobengula

David Lytton

The young, independent nations of Africa control many valuable underground resources. Yet few can match the grandeur and mystery of the treasure of Lobengula, last king of the Matabele, an offshoot of the Zulu nation. Lobengula's vast fortune still lies in a secret burial ground. Many adventurers, including the author's father, made sustained and desperate efforts to find the Lobengula fortune. Protected by the dangers of nature, and by a mysterious curse, the treasure of Lobengula has yet to be found.

In a particular spot in Africa, near a tributary of the Zambezi, lies a hoard of gold, diamonds, and ivory which in 1893 was valued at three million pounds sterling. It was the insurance policy amassed by Lobengula, chief of the Matabele people, and it still is available to their descendants, for it never has been unearthed. A number of historians of Rhodesian affairs have scorned or doubted the existence of this treasure, but of course the evidence for it would not be a matter of public record.

Lobengula was the last king of the Matabele, an offshoot of the Zulu nation, and one of the most accommodating to the intrusion of the white strangers. Better than any other great African despot he understood that the white intruder not only had more powerful forces at his command but he was better established as an individual to cope with natural disturbances such as epidemics, droughts, and plagues. Lobengula was one of the few Africans willing to learn from the whites and to assist them, provided he did not lose sovereignty over his own tribal lands and was treated with sufficient respect.

The chieftain, a tall imposing gentleman, naked except for a roll of blue cloth around his waist, was described by Sir Sydney Shippard, Commissioner of the Bechuanaland Protectorate, who said: "Lobengula walks quite erect with his head thrown back and his broad chest expanded, and as he marches along at a slow pace with his long staff in his right hand while all the men around shout his praises, he looks the part to perfection."

He was a tyrant in the tradition of his father and of the tribal customs that had selectively raised his people above others in the southern continent. Quick death was a small price to pay for regimental insubordination or incivility. Excruciating torture at the hands of the witch doctors was a more frequent penalty for misdemeanor. After he had accepted white emissaries seeking mining concessions, which he granted, he entered into a quaint correspondence, through the usual channels, with Queen Victoria. He thought the good queen equivalent in power to himself and that she would have as many husbands as he had wives, but this was one of the many illusions he was led to discard by continual contact with the white man. The queen replied that she was greatly distressed to learn he had 300 wives and wondered whether this number could be reduced. To please her and to demonstrate his good intentions he limited himself to a mere 150. The other 150 had their throats cut, since a king's wife could not cohabit with a commoner.

Lobengula understood mining; he understood what was happening farther south at Kimberley and on the Witwatersrand and sent his young men to work in the mines. They brought back to him specimens of what they were digging, and these he carefully stored away. Also, concession hunters bargained for his favors and paid him in ready cash for signed documents granting exclusive prospecting rights in particular areas. Also, like his father, he was engaged in the ivory trade and knew its value. He dealt with the white man on almost equal economic terms and realized quite soon that the white man was rapacious and that he could not win against him. His correspondence with Sir Leander Starr Jameson, the Scottish physician, statesman, and associate of Cecil Rhodes, with Rhodes himself, and with delegates of Sir Henry Loch, High Commissioner in South Africa from 1889 to 1895, bear witness to this. Lobengula took all he could knowing that eventually he would have to get out.

Rhodes was an impatient man dragged down by an aneurism of the aorta that made him look blue and puffy. He knew it would kill him before his ambition to paint the map of Africa a British red from the Cape to Cairo could be accomplished. He had overplayed his hand in opening what is now Rhodesia and had made extravagant promises of loot and land to the Pioneer Corps who were to claim it for the Chartered Company he had floated under the most noble auspices.

Lobengula could not contain his young braves, who resented any limitation to their raiding. The Matabele war of 1893 followed, and before the British could bring him to personal submission Lobengula left his capital, Bulawayo, with a train of ox wagons. He had been as conciliatory to the pressures of the white man surrounding him as anyone could be, but the white establishment was in the control of that peculiar fomenter of trouble, Dr. Jameson. Finally, when the king wrote from his heart, "What great wrong have I done? Tell me," Jameson did not answer. Lobengula trekked away with his wagons and a few of his wives, his witch doctor and counselors and a few of his tribesmen to find a new land—as his grandfather had done when escaping from the great Shaka the Zulu. It was a mark of his tribe to return northwards.

He was harried by patrols sent out by Jameson, who had two objectives in mind: to recover the treasure in order to back up the Chartered Company's exchequer and to bring the rest of the Matabele to heel by securing the king's surrender. Lobengula not only evaded them but sent a messenger with a bag containing a hundred pounds in gold sovereigns to request peace and a meeting. The messenger was murdered, the bag stolen. Two troopers later were court-martialed but by then Lobengula was dead.

He died of fever in 1894 and was elaborately buried with his treasure, as was customary. The witch doctor selected the site, sent half a troop forward to excavate it and inter the body and treasure, sent in the other half to slaughter the excavators and bury them around the site to guard the king's spirit, placed a mighty curse on the disturbers of the grave in perpetuity, and brought back the remaining tribesmen to an appointed place where they were slaughtered by the rest of the tribe, so that only the witch doctor knew the precise place of burial.

Rhodes' agents made determined attempts to find this site, and the witch doctor was harried for the rest of his life—as was his son Sibanda. Then greater issues arose to occupy southern Africa—the Boer War, the Union, the rebellion against joining Britain in the First World War.

But in 1914 South Africa agreed to neutralize German South West Africa and General Jan Smuts and Louis Botha took it over in a matter of months, the first Allied victory. In this campaign my father, Maj. J. G. W. Leipoldt, was intelligence officer for General Smuts and while sifting through the German official files came across a slim folder containing a sketched map, survey reckonings, a list of payments for transport, and some papers in code. After some calculation it was clear the maps referred to territory not under German occupation. But the code eluded him and he set the folder aside until he could get a further clue. Shortly afterward he accompanied Smuts on the East African campaign and it was here, while interrogating two Africans recruited by the Germans, that he learned they had accompanied a party of Germans "from far away" into Rhodesia before the war. What had they gone to Rhodesia for? To look for a place. What place? A king's place. They knew no more than that.

On his next leave my father went to Rhodesia and there heard the Lobengula story from the Matabele remnants, heard how he had died and the ingenious plans for the burial of his body and his treasure against the day when the white man should go and the Matabele regain their land and status.

The witch doctor had died some four years after Lobengula's death, and his son made his way south to the Cape. But in a country of bounty hunters he was seldom far ahead of those who were anxious to get his secret. He actually was imprisoned for a time but adopted the ruse of being insane and a missionary intervened to get him released. He settled down in the early 1900s at another mission station where he learned to read and write.

After the 1914–18 war my father returned to his occupation as government land surveyor, taking the German file with him. Eventually he cracked the code and as he had come to suspect, the papers referred to an attempt to discover the Lobengula treasure. With Teutonic thoroughness the papers set out all the known facts derived from interrogations, with descriptions and names of the witch doctor and his son and their last known whereabouts. By fateful coincidence the mission at which the son had sought shelter was the one where my father had been brought up. In 1920 my father finally traced him and he seemed prepared to tell my father what he knew. But the years and the drink he had taken to console his plight had fuddled his mind; he could not be precise as to the exact location. What he did remember vividly was the system of markers devised around the site to pinpoint the place.

By deduction, guesswork, and intuition my father narrowed the area down to some thirty square miles and at the end of 1920 organized a small expedition to explore it. He recruited local Matabele as porters and diggers but after a fortnight spent traversing the area they became suspicious and demanded to know what he was looking for. He felt obliged to tell them. That night they all melted away into the bush, leaving him alone with equipment and stores which had to be abandoned.

Two years later my father set out again, this time engaging his porters in South West Africa, making a long and circuitous safari across Africa. He himself traveled in an old Model T Ford. He was now much clearer about the likely location. One small drawback was that his calculations placed it across the border in Portuguese territory and he could not obtain a prospecting license from the Portuguese authorities. However, it was wild uninhabited country and he took a chance of getting across and working unobserved.

He later described the first indication he had that he had found the place—an unnatural silence in the bush. There was no birdsong, no movement, no indication of animal life.

"It was about midday," he wrote. "We all came to a halt. The porters put down their loads and were plainly afraid. Some stood holding hands. It was unnatural and eerie. I went ahead alone and to my intense excitement saw the markers exactly as Sibanda had described them to me. Where their lines coordinated I prodded into the soil and sure enough struck solid rock."

With him was one other white man, a hunter called Bezuidenhout whose gun supplied meat for the expedition. "Bezuidenhout knew nothing of Lobengula and wholly accepted my story of diamond prospecting, but from his deep bush instinct he declared the place accursed and that night said to me, 'Something very strange has taken place here. It is not a good place.' And that night for the first time the porters did not sing around their fires but sat huddled together in silence. When I slept I dreamed of swarms of flies, which in native mythology is an indication of death."

The next day they started digging but the work came to a halt when they unearthed two of the skeletons with broken legs set to guard the king's spirit. The men would not go on; they wanted to go home. When they were persuaded that home was over 1,000 miles away and they could not make it without maps and guidance, they returned to work, but that evening Bezuidenhout, a careful and accomplished hunter, was killed half a mile from the camp by a lion. The porters now jabbered that the place had a curse on it and nothing would hold them there. "I had come to feel it myself and felt I was tampering with something beyond my powers of comprehension but nevertheless real and evil. I told them to pack. We left at dawn."

However, my father could not overcome his obsession with the place and three years later went back again. On this occasion he had brought along a variety of charms and amulets and at the first sign of fear he arranged these with some ceremony around the place to assuage his men. But again an accident intervened. One of the Y-shaped trenches inexplicably collapsed, burying ten men.

"How that trench crumbled I shall never know, but again, the night before, I had dreamed of swarms of flies. We had got to the undoubted burial chamber. I was sick at heart but nothing would keep those poor devils there a moment longer. And I myself came down with fever and we had a terrible journey which I only half remember as a haunted delirium."

Nevertheless he made one more attempt in 1934. By now his purpose was widely known and while actually at work on the site he was confounded to learn of claims made to a share in the treasure should it be found. The Portuguese demanded 50 percent, since it was in their territory. The DeBeers Mining Company required 75 percent on the ground that the diamonds and nuggets had been stolen from their diggings. The London Mission Society put in for 50 percent since the treasure rightly belonged to the Matabele and the LMS felt themselves trustees for that tribe.

"It was unbelievable and I saw years of litigation stretching before me, one more sign of that damned curse in which I do now profoundly believe. There was only one decent thing to do, fill in the trenches and restore the place to what it had been. I was tempted also to remove the markers, but who knows, the Matabele might one day come into their own and this little hoard would start them off very well."

My father destroyed his papers and left the place for good. Strangely enough the following year two men who had discovered a copy of the German folder in Berlin and had been working along the same lines flew out to South Africa to mount an expedition. They never set foot in the country. Their plane nosedived into the sea within sight of the land.

As far as I know only one person now knows the exact location but nothing would induce him to tempt the effects of the curse in which he too "profoundly believes."

The Magnificence of Baalbek

Arnold L. Kent

The civil war that has raged in Lebanon has made the magnificent ruins of Baalbek less accessible than ever. Thus we are no nearer to the answer posed by the imposing ruin of this ancient Phoenician city. Baal was one of the pagan gods denounced in the Bible, and a tremendous stone acropolis bears witness to the wealth and impact which Baal worship controlled. Hundreds of years before the birth of Christ, the people of Canaan built and inhabited this thriving town—until the sands of time, and unknown fates, turned it into one of the world's most imposing ruins.

Baalbek, a modern resort town in Lebanon, conceals an age-old mystery which will puzzle men forever, for the early history of this ancient Canaanite city is lost in time. Many hundreds of years before the birth of Christ its name derived from the Canaanites' worship of Baal, a god they apparently considered the most important in the pantheon.

In Old Testament days the city lay just east of the Lebanon mountains near that part of Canaan the Greeks called Phoenicia. This nation was a strip of land about 200 miles long and 35 miles at its widest along the eastern

Mediterranean coast. Some of the stonework at Baalbek has been attributed to the Phoenicians, so it must have been one of their frontier cities. It was a thriving trade center when Greece occupied it in 311 B.C. and renamed it Heliopolis (city of the sun), but unfortunately the earliest reliable records stem from Roman times in the first century of the Christian era.

Baalbek's greatest landmark is a tremendous stone acropolis which rises more than 40 feet above the ground at the city's edge. This platform measures about 400 feet wide and 880 feet long and is supported by blocks of stone which were quarried a half mile away. The lower courses are made of moderate-sized blocks but these grow in size on each succeeding tier. Three of the monoliths at the 20-foot level are so huge that even given the tools of modern technology we cannot understand how they moved them intact.

These awesome blocks are 63 to 64 feet long, 13 feet high, and 10 feet thick. Each is as large as a three-room house and weighs about 1,000 tons—two million pounds of solid rock. It is said one block contains enough material to build a house 60 feet square and 40 feet high with walls a foot thick.

Our largest railway cars and hoisting cranes are too puny to handle such monoliths. A large modern overhead crane will lift about 400 tons, and our largest freight car can transport 110 tons at freight-train speed. But it would take three of our largest cranes to hoist one of Baalbek's stones and it would have to be done in such a way that the block wouldn't be damaged by the stress of its own tremendous weight. So far as we know the men of ancient Baalbek had only their muscles, draft animals, and a few primitive tools. How did they transport these huge blocks and lift them into position?

Wheeled vehicles were used in the Middle East as early as 2000 B.C. but it is doubtful they could have transported the blocks. Even if somehow one could be maneuvered onto a wheeled conveyance the mighty load would drive the wheels into the ground or grind them to pieces on the rocky surface.

An even larger block still lies partly hewn in the nearby

quarry, giving rise to speculation that the citizens of Baalbek suffered a sudden misfortune that brought their work to an unexpected halt. It seems we never will know how the first three gigantic stones were transported nor why the fourth one wasn't.

A massive migration of Semitic Amorites took place in the Middle East about 4,500 years ago. Some of the Canaanites who were part of this migration settled along the coasts of Lebanon and Palestine. In time the coastal Canaanites were dubbed "Phoenicians" by the Greeks, probably because of the excellent Tyrian purple dye they were manufacturing and selling. "Phoenicia" is believed to be a derivative of the Greek *phoinike*, which means purple-red. This expensive dye, which took its name from the city of Tyre, was so highly valued that purple became an international symbol of royalty and remains so today.

Phoenicia, the first major civilization in Lebanon, considered itself a single nation but it never became a unified independent state. Instead it consisted of a number of city-states maintaining a homogeneous civilization by taking turns dominating each other through the centuries. Each king ruled by divine right, but his power was limited by a council of elders made up of sea captains, merchants, and heads of aristocratic families. Baalbek is 35 miles from the coast and probably was one of Phoenicia's smaller city-states.

The people of early Baalbek were Caucasians of medium height with thin lips and broad, sometimes hooked noses. They had thick hair, straight or frizzy, and their skin tone ranged from light to dark brown. They rode in iron-clad chariots and dressed in fine embroidered fabrics dyed in all shades of purple from blue to dull crimson.

Although the Phoenicians could work hard and endure great hardships they also loved luxury and ease. The common people lived in well-built closely packed buildings of several stories each, and the residences of the nobility were large and extravagantly furnished. All the splendid cities of Phoenicia were built by slave labor, and the body of a human sacrifice usually was embedded in the foundation of each city's main gate.

These early Phoenicians must have suffered from skin diseases and eye problems because of the dust, the flies, and the glare of a tropical sun. But they could correct at least one of the physical discomforts that still plagues all mankind—the wealthy citizens of Baalbek wore some of the first dentures in history. They were not exactly false teeth. Instead of carving artificial biting and chewing surfaces the Phoenicians extracted teeth from slaves as they were needed and fitted them into their own mouths with gold wire.

They were not particularly inventive but as highly skilled craftsmen they improved on the techniques of other nations—for instance, the art of glassblowing. This old Egyptian science was improved and further developed in the Phoenician cities of Tyre and Sidon.

The farmers of Baalbek grew a variety of crops—grain, grapes, oranges, olives, mulberries, and timber trees. The Cedars of Lebanon have been world-famous for centuries.

The religion of the Phoenicians was a kind of nature worship aimed at controlling the seasons, and it made fearsome demands on them. In times of crises the firstborn babies of several families, some crops, and the domestic animals were sacrificed to appease their pagan gods. The Phoenicians were cruel and fearless and without ideals. They respected no one's rights, certainly not those of the weak. Yet these same barbaric people enjoyed the gentle sounds of the zither.

The holy men of Baalbek danced and shouted themselves into a frenzy, muttering gibberish and performing wild antics. The people then believed the dervish was possessed by a god who was speaking to them through the holy man's mouth. In more sober moments these holy men could predict the future, find lost valuables, and give sage advice to believers.

The Phoenicians became the finest shipbuilders and seamen of their time, and it was they who opened the oceans of the world to international trade. Their discovery of celestial navigation made it safe to sail at night and thus made seamanship profitable. The 27th chapter of the biblical book of *Ezekiel* pays tribute to their seamanship and their merchandising techniques.

Through their mastery of the sea the Phoenicians became middlemen and distributors of luxury goods and grew wealthy. All the known world became their marketplace. The coastal cities of Tyre, Sidon, and Byblos became world centers. Baalbek, linked directly to Tyre by camel caravan, also must have prospered.

Overland trade routes brought goods to Baalbek from the exotic East and from Armenia in the north. Not only were the Assyrians and Babylonians Phoenicia's customers, but they allowed her camel caravans free passage through their lands as far as the Persian Gulf. Baalbek's merchants sold everything from Asian slaves to Spanish metals. The city's horses, mules, and asses came from Armenia in what is now Turkey. And Phoenician traders, wrapped in fur and leather garments as protection against the extreme cold, crossed the mountains on them because camels could not travel over such rough terrain.

Merchandising was Phoenicia's greatest source of wealth, but its people were unexcelled craftsmen in other industries as well. Their glassware, fabrics, dyes, leather, ivory, and metal products were in great demand. Also, they had learned stone masonry from the Egyptians during the thirteenth and twelfth centuries B.C. Although the pyramids were already ancient perhaps the construction methods used to build them were not forgotten and the Egyptians taught Baalbek's artisans how to handle the immense blocks used to create the city's acropolis.

It was the Phoenicians who helped King Solomon build the Temple of Jerusalem. He asked Hiram, King of Tyre, for help because "there is not among us any that can skill to hew timber like unto the Sidonians." (Old Testament Sidonians were Phoenicians.) Thus it happened that Phoenician masons and carpenters joined Solomon's work force to build a temple of timber and stone. Some of the timber well may have come from the forests on the slopes of the Lebanon and Anti-Lebanon mountains near the valley where Baalbek lies.

Phoenician industrial genuis seems to have had no end. When the iron age began and with it came the development of metal tools the Phoenicians reasoned that their business would be drastically increased. So they invented a simpler method of keeping accounts and gave the world its first phonetic alphabet. Now they could record their entire language by simply repeating twenty-two letters, just as we now repeat twenty-six. Prior to this brilliant innovation every word had been represented more or less by its own character, which resulted in a cumbersome collection of hieroglyphics.

Unfortunately the Phoenicians never used this spectacular tool to record their own history. They left fewer records than any other ancient nation because they were interested only in keeping the accounts of their widespread economy. Everything we know about them comes from the writings of their customers and neighbors.

However, the Greeks, who always had been students of Phoenicia, were quick to adapt the new alphabet to their own language. In turn the Romans picked it up and soon it had spread throughout the known world, becoming the basis for all phonetic alphabets. Only in the Orient, geographically isolated from direct Phoenician influence, did the ancient pictograph form of writing prevail, persisting there to this day.

Despite Phoenicia's accomplishments a strain of sadness runs through its history. The people who gave the world its alphabet were guilty of the most corrupt, vicious, and depraved human conduct in all history. The people of Canaan were so wicked that "the Lord rained upon Sodom and Gomorrah brimstone and fire from the Lord of Heaven."

Scholars believe that five towns known as the "Cities of the Plain" had been scheduled for destruction. They were Sodom, Gomorrah, Admah, Zeboim, and Zoar. But Zoar was saved when Lot asked God to spare the city so he could hide there (*Genesis 19*). The remainder of the Canaanite cities which spread from Gaza in the south to where Tripoli now stands also were spared—Baalbek was one of them.

As the centuries marched by Phoenicia fell to nation after nation. The Assyrians, Egyptians, Babylonians and Persians all took turns governing this amazing people. Yet somehow they managed to retain their skills and customs. Not until 331 B.C. when Alexander the Great took Phoenicia from the Persians did the citizens of Baalbek begin to lose their separate identity. After that they gradually were absorbed into the Greco-Macedonian Empire—but even this was not their end. Coins were minted in the Phoenician language as late as the third century A.D., hundreds of years after the civilization really had come to an end. The genius, daring, and skill of the Phoenicians was a long time dying.

The city of Baalbek attained its greatest splendor while it was part of Rome's Syrian colony. Roman domination began in 64 B.C. when Pompey invaded the Middle East. A few decades later Emperor Augustus garrisoned troops in Baalbek, and amid the already ancient ruins Rome began to build and dedicate temples to its own gods. Rome's three magnificent temples in Baalbek often are described as the most imposing and beautiful in the Roman world, unexcelled by any in Rome itself.

Two of the temples—dedicated to Jupiter and Bacchus—were constructed on Baalbek's huge acropolis. The acropolis itself consists of four main sections which give it a slightly irregular shape. The first section a visitor encounters is the impressive entranceway and forecourt. This monumental gateway is a partially enclosed rectangular building which originally had a colonnade 165 feet wide flanked by two square towers that rose nearly 100 feet into the air. Inscriptions on the bases of three of these columns tell us that the temple complex was erected to the great gods of Heliopolis by Antoninus and Caracalla.* Three doors lead from the gateway into a hexagonal forecourt which once was surrounded by an exquisite hexagonal colonnade. A series of alcoves still decorate four of the court's six sides.

Three more doorways, now lying in ruins, led from the forecourt into the Great Court or Court of the Altar. This huge area, the central and largest section of the acropolis, is about 370 feet wide and 440 feet long and more than 20 feet above ground level.

*Two Roman emperors of the early Christian era. Antonius Pius ruled from 138 to 161 A. D. and Caracalla from 211 to 217 A. D.

The square and semicircular alcoves that adorn three sides of the Great Court were designed as resting places for worshipers. Each has a number of now-empty niches where statues once stood. A colonnade of polished Egyptian granite, no longer standing, once separated the alcoves from the court. Broken columns and fragments of the elaborately carved entablature lie scattered around the court.

The ruins of a large altar can be seen near the center of the Great Court with a cleansing or absolution basin on either side. This may have been one of the sites where Canaanite priests sacrificed human victims to heathen deities in Old Testament times. The altar was badly damaged in the fourth century when the Great Court was filled with earth so that a Christian basilica could be built over it. The basilica later was demolished during the excavation of the ruins.

A flight of wide steps led from the Great Court to the third section of the acropolis, the temple terrace proper, more than 40 feet above the ground. The temple that stood there was dedicated to Rome's supreme deity Jupiter—known to the Greeks as Zeus. The Temple of Jupiter, also called the Great Temple and the Temple of the Sun, was 300 feet long, 170 feet wide, and more than 80 feet high—considerably larger than Athens' Parthenon. It seems fitting that a shrine built for Rome's greatest god should incorporate what must be man's largest building blocks. The huge monoliths described earlier are part of the wall surrounding the temple terrace.

More than fifty Corinthian columns, each consisting of three huge stone drums, once adorned the Temple of Jupiter. Six of these still stand in an unbroken row—all that's left of the structure. They measure 7½ feet in diameter and tower 65 feet above the temple floor. Reputedly they are the tallest columns in the world and still hold aloft the remnant of an elaborately carved three-layered entablature. A rain gutter in the cornice channeled water into a series of beautifully carved lion heads spaced at intervals around this entablature. In heavy rains water gushed from the lions' jaws in a symbolic roar.

The great Temple of Jupiter was destroyed when it was

mined by the Christians for material to build the basilica over the altar. Before earthquake, time, and man reduced it to rubble it must have been a magnificent structure.

Across from the Great Temple a part of the acropolis juts out into an L-shape. Here stands a temple dedicated to Jupiter's son Bacchus, whom the Greeks knew as Dionysus—he who gave King Midas his golden touch.

Youngest of the Greek deities, Bacchus originally was the god of planting and fruitfulness, especially of vineyards. He gradually evolved into the god of wine and traveled the world teaching the art of cultivating the vines and making wine.

Naturally, worship of the god of wine took the form of drunken parties. Religious rites dedicated to Bacchus grew progressively more depraved over the centuries until 168 B.C. when the Roman Senate outlawed the immoralities of these dionysia or orgia. From these festivities comes our word "orgy."

However, some good came from the drunken melees that were held in Bacchus' honor. They gave us our theater. Greek tragedy as an art form arose from the dithyrambic songs sung to Bacchus during spring nature festivals. In the beginning all the celebrants joined in the singing. Then the bolder ones began jumping to the tops of altars and sacrificial tables to sing lyrics which were echoed by the others. Thus was born the chorus. Thus the theatrical stage we know today evolved from altar and sacrificial table.

Baalbek's well-preserved Temple of Bacchus, built about 150 A.D., is much smaller than the Temple of Jupiter. It is about 57 feet high with inside dimensions of only 75 by 85 feet. But small as it is, many authorities consider this temple the most beautiful Roman monument in Lebanon.

The temple is entered through a huge doorway—four stories high and more than 20 feet wide. Vertical strips elaborately decorated with carvings of Bacchus and other mythical beings adorn the doorjambs. Interlaced with these figures are grapevines, clusters of fruit, poppies, and ears of wheat, fitting tributes to the god of planting and fruitfulness. The entire surface of the exterior of the lintel also is exquisitely carved—although it now is broken into four pieces which are wedged precariously in place above the open doorway.

Fluted columns on each side of the doorway form a prostyle or portico. Beyond these are plain columns 52 feet tall that are part of a peristyle that runs around the building, 10 feet from the walls. However, more than half of the 46 columns have fallen.

While the walls of the temple remain almost perfectly preserved, the roof is gone. Although the exterior surfaces are quite plain the stones were carefully dressed. The joints fit together so perfectly that a knife blade cannot be inserted between them at any point except where the wall is damaged.

Two rows of statue niches, one above the other, run the full length of the interior walls, which are divided by fluted columns that do not stand free. The statue of Bacchus that must have stood at the western end of the temple is no longer there.

The third structure—the Temple of Venus—is not on the acropolis but rather stands at ground level 1,000 feet away nestling close to the modern village of Baalbek. Dedicated to the Greco-Roman goddess of love, this circular structure is the smallest of the three Roman temples. Originally it had a domed stone roof supported by six Grecian granite columns. This temple, ornamented in much the same manner as the two on the acropolis, is believed to date from about 250 A.D. The Temple of Venus was the last major structure erected in ancient Baalbek.

Modern Baalbek is a popular resort town of 9,000 people, famous for its summer festivals in which top theatrical companies appear each July and August. A group of excavators inspired this tradition fifty years ago when they took to reciting poetry during their rest periods. They found that peculiar acoustical conditions in the ruins amplified the ring of their voices. Today people come from all over the world to enjoy the festivals and to be awed by the immensity of the mighty acropolis—and the secret it holds.

Perhaps the mystery of Baalbek never can be satisfactorily resolved. Nothing we understand or believe today can help us rationalize the huge stones in the acropolis. But there is a sort of answer. . . .

The biblical book of *Numbers* tells the story of Moses leading the children of Israel through the wilderness. One day the Lord told Moses, "Send thou men, that they may search the land of Canaan, which I give unto the children of Israel. . . ."

Moses sent some of his tribal leaders to scout this promised land. They searched for forty days, spying on all the tribes of the land, including "the Canaanites (who) dwell by the sea." (These were the Phoenicians.)

Upon their return only one of them, Caleb of Judah, told the people that they should attack at once, saying the land easily could be taken.

His fellow spies disagreed, saying, "We be not able to go up against the people; for they are stronger than we. . . .

"The land, through which we have gone to search it, is a land that eateth up the inhabitants thereof; and all the people that we saw in it are men of a great stature.

"And there we saw the giants, the sons of Anak, which come of the giants: and we were in our own sight as grasshoppers, and so we were in their sight."

Two-million-pound building blocks seem about right for giants such as these.

Riddle of the
Nazca Drawings
Sharon S. McKern

Who were the Indians who lived in Peru, more than a thousand years ago, and whose giant earth drawings have survived to this day? Some of the deep etchings have geometric designs, others are huge drawings of animals, such as birds, monkeys, and spiders. As Sharon McKern notes, some of the designs, "lace back and forth across the landscape," or as "giant circles" and "mysteriously radiating lines." The designs are in remote areas, and they cover so much ground that for the most part they can only be seen fully from the air. The questions remain: Who made these drawings, and what do they mean?

To those who investigate the American past, few pre-Columbian peoples are so intriguing as those of Inca Peru. The Incas had no wheeled vehicles. Their knowledge of animal domestication was severely limited. For beasts of burden they had only the llama and alpaca, suitable for relatively light loads. They domesticated only the guinea pig for food. As far as we know, they lacked even a rudimentary written language.

And yet they established what was perhaps the most sophisticated and well-organized government in all the New World. The vast Inca Empire, ruled by a living god, stretched along the Andes for more than 2,500 miles ranging from the southernmost boundaries of Colombia to the Maule River in central Chile. Armies of workers using tools of stone and bronze accomplished feats of engineering unsurpassed even today. Trained relay runners formed a human communications network linking the Inca capital with its far-flung outposts. Irrigation canals and agricultural terraces brought millions of acres of land into active production.

Some of these canals and terraces are in use today, after a span of four centuries. Many of the well-built Inca roads, although too narrow for use by modern jeeps or automobiles, are traveled with ease and frequency by the present-day inhabitants of the region. Beneath the rubble of Spanish colonial structures toppled by earthquakes rest the undamaged foundations of Inca walls and dwellings. And from the tombs of pre-Columbian Peru come perfectly preserved Inca mummies wrapped in fine bright-colored textiles that have withstood the ravages of time. To gaze upon such remnants of the Inca Empire is to arrest time and capture brief glimpses into a romantic past. Little wonder, then, that this great native empire holds such fascination for those who probe American prehistory.

The Inca civilization represented the culmination of thousands of years of cultural and intellectual development in Peru. The Incas were comparative latecomers, rising to power less than a century before the Spanish Conquest. They were preceded by diverse fragmented Indian tribes whose complex histories are lost in time. Among these early inhabitants of Peru were little-known desert peoples who raised remarkably high cultures centuries before the birth of the first Inca king.

To the west of the Andes is a barren, inhospitable desert that runs some 2,000 miles along the coast of Peru. This is a region of intense heat. Much of the desert is totally devoid of life and to the modern visitor it seems incredible that man could wrest a living from this harsh environment.

Fog occasionally crowds in from the coastal waters but rain never falls here. There are, however, small rivers and streams that carry water to the sea from the forested slopes of the Andes, where rains are torrential. Through tedious and painstaking techniques of irrigation, crops can be grown here, and where food can be grown, people can survive.

In the northern range of the coastal desert lived a hardy warlike people known as the Mochicas. About A.D. 200, Mochica peoples formed a loose confederacy of groups living in adjoining valleys. Our knowledge of their culture comes primarily from the pottery they buried with their dead.

The Mochicas were skilled sculptors, modeling in clay the forms they had seen or fantasied. Among the pottery recovered from desert excavations in northern Peru are vessels shaped like fish, owls, deer, monkeys, birds, frogs, and fierce fanged gods. There are human forms, too, and clay portraits so masterfully executed that they are startling in their realism. Not only the usual but also the bizarre caught the attention of Mochica sculptors. The pottery they left behind includes grotesque representations of disease and physical deformity—and graphic portrayals of human sexual activity. Ancient Mochica pottery is abundant in modern collections of pornographic art.

Painted vessels give us heady glimpses into the daily lives of the Mochicas. On their smooth brightly colored surfaces are represented people from all walks of Mochica life. There are chiefs, merchants, craftsmen, mothers, warriors, hunters, weavers and musicians—all dressed in suitable costume and engaged in appropriate activity.

Near the center of Peru's coastal desert, predating Mochica culture by nearly two centuries, flourished another unique Indian race. They were the Paracas, known primarily for their extraordinary textiles and exquisite embroidered garments. Miraculously preserved by the arid desert air these are as vivid today as they were when first woven. Like the Incas who came later, the Paracas venerated their dead. The mummies of chiefs, priests and honored noblemen were wrapped first in plain cotton shrouds, then enveloped in yards of fine beautifully woven fabric; tucked deep within the mummy wrappings were offerings of food and gold. Archaeologists have recovered several hundred Paracas mummies. At one site alone—Paracas

Necropolis—excavators unearthed more than four hundred seated mummies, all elaborately prepared and preserved for posterity.

But it is to the south of the Paracas region that we find the remains of the most mysterious of Peru's desert kingdoms. Across the southern coast, about 250 miles from Lima, the Rio Grande River branches out into eight small tributaries. These are dry for more than half the year; nevertheless, there is sufficient water to irrigate the intervening valleys and thus support their small populations of from one thousand to three thousand people.

Between the Nazca and the Ica valleys, from about A.D. 200 to 600, lived an enigmatic Indian race believed to be responsible for the most large scale of all archaeological riddles. In one of the world's driest deserts—and for reasons we may never uncover—the Ica-Nazcas carefully etched into the earth's surface great networks of lines and geometric figures.

Some of the tracings are ruler-straight, running along the desert plains for distances of up to five miles; some continue along for no more than a few feet. Others form immense geometric figures—squares, rectangles, trapezoids, triangles—that measure thousands of feet in width. Still others trace the outlines of birds, plants, monkeys, spiders, and other creatures or loop around and around in dizzying, seemingly meaningless spirals. One figure, found near a huge trapezoid located close by the Pan-American Highway, consists of a gigantic pair of hands—with but nine fingers.

Most of the geometric figures are neatly arranged, their borders clearly and concisely outlined. Other lines lace back and forth across the landscape chaotically overlapping in places, as if they were etched at different times by artists with different interests. There are giant circles, too, and mysterious radiating lines.

The Spanish never mentioned these curious markings in any of their writings. And present-day inhabitants of the region, although aware of the tracings, can shed no light on the mystery. Apparently, the secret of these vast drawings was buried with the people who made them. One Spanish chonicler, Cieza de León, mentions in his writings that all of the Indians of the Nazca Valley died in the civil wars that wreaked havoc on the region as rival Spanish armies battled for possession of New World lands and Indian slaves.

Modern inhabitants of the Nazca Valley as well as tourists who fly over the area refer to the desert etchings as "Inca roads." And from both air and ground the majority of the markings look very much like roads or light-colored trails edged with darker filaments at either border.

Yet the lines predate the Incas by centuries and could not have been used for ordinary transportation. Most begin and end seemingly nowhere. A true Inca road, built shortly before the Spanish Conquest, runs directly across some of the larger desert figures; the Incas, at least, were totally indifferent to these strange sand drawings.

Both lines and figures appear to have been made by the simple process of removing surface pebbles to expose the lighter soil below. Surface material was then piled along either side of the line. Rocks and gravel on the desert's surface are dark; they contain iron which oxidizes and darkens on contact with the air—hence the clarity of these prehistoric constructions. A single heavy rainfall would wash away the coat of dust that clings to the rocky outlines of these gigantic forms. But because it seldom rains in the Nazca Valley the fragile etchings have survived for centuries.

The Nazca markings are so immense that their true shapes can be ascertained only from the air. Some of the more complex networks cover an area more than forty miles long and ten miles wide.

Why did prehistoric peoples labor under the broiling sun to devise these giant figures? How could designs be executed with such precision by peoples who could never view their own handiwork?

When first observed from the air, the Nazca tracings were laughingly called "prehistoric landing strips," and compared to the "canals" on Mars. In 1939 one scholar—Mejia Xesspe—suggested that the desert lines represent ceremonial paths. Eight years later Prof. Hans Horkheimer theorized that the lines might have served in prehistoric times to link the graves of members of local families or clans. But no graves have ever been found at the junctures of these connecting lines.

In 1941, an imaginative American historian stumbled upon the most promising clue so far—one that may one day unravel the secret of the mysterious markings. In June of that year, Paul Kosok, then a professor of history at Long Island University in New York, traveled to Peru to study the prehistoric irrigation systems of the northwest coast and their possible relationships with important ruins of the past. With his wife Dr. Kosok pored over aerial photographs of the region and then decided to explore the so-called Inca roads in the hope that they might represent—or lead to—prehistoric irrigation canals.

Quickly the Kosoks ruled out the possibility that the tracings had anything to do with irrigation. The lines often ran over small desert hillocks; water in such "canals" would have had to defy the law of gravity. Further, the markings had no physical connection with known rivers, which connection would have been mandatory for any system of irrigation canals.

Even so, the Kosoks continued to explore the region, now thoroughly intrigued by the desert markings. They chose a wide Nazca line that crossed the modern Pan-American Highway to the south of Palpa and followed it on foot as it led straight up one side of a small desert mesa.

There the line came to an abrupt end. But it was surrounded by several similar lines that—together with longer, narrower ones—radiated from a center near which the Kosoks stood.

From this vantage point, Dr. Kosok and his wife commanded a clear view of the horizon and the surrounding landscape, which was crisscrossed by the huge rectangles and trapezoids typical in the Nazca Valley. They walked to the center of the radiating lines and stood together, watching the setting of the sun.

Then—in one of those rare and wonderful coincidences that sometimes bless one science or another—the sun set almost exactly over the end of one of the long Nazca lines.

A moment later the Kosoks recalled that the date was

June 22, the day of the winter solstice in the southern hemisphere—the day when the sun sets farthest north of due west.

Had the peoples of the Nazca Valley etched this line into the desert to mark the winter solstice? If so, did the other strange tracing also represent astronomical events meaningful to the peoples of Peru's coastal desert?

Kosok thought so. As a scholar he had often contemplated the importance of astronomical observations to regulate the agricultural life of primitive societies across the world. He theorized that the Inca-Nazcas, like other agricultural peoples, must have yearned for an understanding of the productive cycle. In response, they apparently developed numerous calendrical systems—based on astronomical observations—to record the changing seasons and to predict the onset of life-sustaining waters.

Kosok visualized here an ancient Indian society dominated by astronomer-priests who supervised the construction of sight lines intended to mark the points of the horizon where the sun rose and set at different times of the year. Such markings served to pinpoint the beginning and end of important periods in agricultural life and permitted the elite priestly class to calculate or predict the coming of important events. From this crude beginning there could develop a well-organized calendar for determining "holy" or "lucky" days for planting or harvesting crops—a matter of vast importance to people dependent on agriculture for their survival.

Ruins of ancient astronomical formations are known from England, northern France, and other parts of the world. None rivals the Nazca tracings in scale, frequency, or complexity.

For Kosok the markings in the coastal desert of Peru represented the "largest astronomy book in the world." He was determined to read it.

In the few remaining weeks he had to spend in Peru, Kosok flew over the entire area, obtaining high-quality aerial photographs and taking directional readings. He located at least a dozen other "radiating centers." Some of the lines had solstitial direction, as he had expected, but many appeared to have other astronomical significance.

Given time, he thought, he could unravel the riddle of the giant Nazca drawings.

Commitments at home called him back to the United States; he would not be able to return to Peru for more than five years. In the meantime, he turned over his information to Dr. Maria Reiche, a Lima-based mathematician-astronomer who had expressed keen interest in his work. Since that time, Dr. Reiche has become a passionate (some say fanatical) advocate of Kosok's original theory.

Dr. Reiche lives for at least part of the year in a simple adobe hut at the edge of the desert where she can observe the rising and setting of the sun over the ancient Nazca lines. In this way, she has managed to verify the solstitial nature of the lines plotted by Kosok. In addition, she has found new correlations between the tracings and many other heavenly bodies. Obviously, the enigmatic desert tracings were not built in a random fashion but were designed to align with specific positions of the sun, moon, stars and planets.

For Maria Reiche the mysterious Nazca drawings represent an immense desert calendar by which these Indains marked the passing of the years. Like Kosok she would find special meaning in a passage by the early Spanish chronicler Cieze de León, who wrote: "These Indians watched the heavens and the signs very constantly." Maria Reiche has done the same.

Dr. Kosok remained in frequent contact through the mails, then returned to Peru to resume his fieldwork in 1948. Once again his time was limited by obligations at home. But until his death in 1959 he continued to collaborate with Dr. Reiche in attempting to organize and interpret the chaotic network of etchings on the surface of Peru's coastal desert. Together they mapped and computed hundreds of astronomical correlations—and walked hundreds of miles to trace the outline of blurred geometric figures.

It is only the beginning. Still to be explored are hundreds of lines and "roads" that are not related to the solstices and equinoxes. These may have served as sight lines for the rising and setting of the moon, planets, or important stars. Or they may not represent sight lines at all, having served instead to connect related astronomical markings.

And the many lines and figures have not yet been satisfactorily dated. Radiocarbon techniques, so often relied upon by archaeologists to determine the age of prehistoric ruins, cannot be applied to stone. So far only one radiocarbon date has emerged from the Nazca sites; this date—A.D. 500—was obtained from the remains of a tree stump found at the end of one of the long narrow lines. There is no way of knowing how long similar etchings had been under construction before this piece of wood was erected as some sort of marker. We know only that the gigantic desert drawings are at least 1,500 years old.

Since the death of Dr. Kosok, Maria Reiche has worked alone. Her devotion to the project is unparalleled, her energy apparently boundless. For nearly thirty years, she has pored over complex aerial photographs, directional readings, and astronomical calculations. Almost single-handedly she has fended off highway engineers and land developers who would destroy the ancient desert tracings. On occasion she has flown strapped to the outside of a low-flying plane in order to take photographs from just the right angle.

And still the mysteries remain. The hundreds of lines which lack astronomical correlations have not been explained. Were these built to represent astronomical configurations not yet considered? Or did they serve as footpaths along which ancient priest-astronomers led religious processions on ceremonial days?

What of the squares, triangles, trapezoids, and rectangles? These immense geometric forms are too precise to result from the accidental crossing of solstitial lines. Could they have served as sacred enclosures in which religious rituals now lost in time were performed? The largest geometric figures measure 500 feet wide and more than 1,000 feet long. Hundreds if not thousands of worshipers could have gathered within their boundaries. Perhaps they were intended as open-air temples; near some of them have been found large stone heaps—possibly the remains of altars. No one has yet excavated these; perhaps they do contain human burials.

Most perplexing, however, are the animal shapes and rambling spirals. These, hundreds of feet in diameter, are found closely associated with a wide Nazca line or geometric figures. Most are formed by a single continuous line or narrow path that loops and twists over the desert's surface to depict some animal figure.

Why would hardworking desert farmers go to such lengths to make immense outlines of whales, spiders, flying pelicans, and other creatures? Do the fantastic animal shapes represent prehistoric totemlike symbols intended to honor some favorite animal spirit? Or were they offerings of art never meant to be seen by man but dedicated instead to the ever watchful Indian gods who looked down upon the earth from their homes in the skies?

And how do the mysterious markings of Nazca relate to similar figures produced by prehistoric peoples in North America? Giant effigies are known here also, from the parched desert near Blythe, Calif., where crude childlike sketches of men and horses sprawl across the landscape. In the Mississippi Valley huge serpentlike earth mounds were constructed by tribes who occupied the area in the centuries before Columbus.

At some time in the distant past did contacts occur between the peoples of North and South America, contacts that permitted the spread of native religious ideas and of techniques used in building sacred constructions? Or are these scattered effigies products of independent invention, the result of homegrown customs whose origins have been lost?

Many of the baffling animal shapes traced across the coastal desert of southern Peru are similar to those found on Ancient Nazca pottery unearthed in the immediate vicinity. If the Ica-Nazcas repeated the same designs again and again, in pottery and across the landscape, the forms must have had great significance to them. But what?

The history of the Nazca markings is yet to be fully reconstructed. We are left with too many unanswered— perhaps unsolvable—questions. Perhaps the long lines did indeed serve to determine the appropriate dates for planting and harvesting of crops. But the curious spirals and puzzling animal shapes are more difficult to explain.

However energetic future investigations in the Nazca Valley, these desert etchings may remain perplexing.

Easter Island: Still Unsolved

Lawrence Madden

The image is huge and forbidding: human heads, roughly carved in stone, that look out upon the seashore of an isolated Pacific island. For generations, explorers and anthropologists have puzzled over the men who created these gigantic idols. But the forbidding, silent creations of a dead civilization seem to have repulsed scholarly investigation and rational explanations. Mr. Madden has painstakingly examined the history and evidence on Easter Island. Despite new and ingenious studies, the island's mystery still eludes final solution.

Easter Island is the loneliest island in the world. It is 2,600 miles from Valparaiso, Chile, to the east, and 2,700 miles from Tahiti to the west. The nearest land to the north and east is the Galapagos archipelago, some 2,000 miles away. Although swept by Antarctic winds from the south, the climate of this triangular volcanic island is temperate.

The island people call their home *Te Pito-te henua,* "The Navel of the World." The nearest land the islanders can see is above them, the moon and the stars. Therefore, living nearest the stars, they know the names of more stars than you or I could name towns and countries in our own world. Their ancestors lined the shores with scores of giant heads, all looking exactly the same. The huge stone faces, with long spaniel ears and cold scowling eyes, seemed to be warning explorers not to land. These great stone faces were topped with red sandstone caps. They were many times taller than the average man and weighed several tons. Who were these early, unknown islanders? Where did they come from? How did they manage to erect statues of such size? And why?

Whoever they were, they navigated thousands of miles of desolate, unknown seas until they found the loneliest little island in the world. There they whetted their adzes and began the creation of one of the most remarkable engineering achievements of ancient times. They apparently feared no attack, for they built no fortresses; instead, they constructed huge terraces upon which to place their statues. When Dutch sailors first explored the island, they found that the natives had no rope, no timber, no beasts of burden, and no wheeled vehicles. How, then, did they manage to construct those colossi, at whose feet they buried their dead? Why did, one day, the sound of the adze on rock fall suddenly silent? Why were hundreds of tools left abandoned and many of the great stone faces left unfinished, while their mysterious sculptors vanished into the world of myth?

What happened on Easter Island?

Before we inquire into the prehistory (i.e., the pre-European history) of Easter Island, let us recall what we do know about their history. It was on Easter Day, 1772, that the Dutchman Jacob Roggeveen, commander of three ships, became the first European to land on the island's shores. He found the remote island covered with a rich, fertile soil, which supported a flourishing society. The islanders were tall, pale-skinned people with red hair. They wore earplugs so heavy that their earlobes often drooped to their shoulders. A clan of aristocratic priests with shaven heads worshiped in front of those massive stone figures which stood on low stone terraces along the coast. The population did not seem pure or unmixed. Some of the natives who came aboard the Dutch ship were dark-skinned and resembled Polynesians from the more eastern islands. The fair-skinned men wore beards.

Apart from the few women who were sent aboard as pleasure offerings, no women were seen during the one-day visit of the Dutch. The sailors did, however, observe the natives praying before their colossal statues, squatting on their feet, their heads bent reverentially, raising and lowering their arms, with palms together. They lit numerous fires before the statues. In the morning, hundreds of fires were burning, while the natives were lying prostrate on the shore, worshiping the sunrise.

A great many natives went about completely naked, their bodies tattooed in a continuous design of birds and strange figures. Some had feathered crowns, others wore hats made of reed. Still others wore cloaks of bark cloth, colored yellow and red. They lived in long, low huts made of reeds, which looked like upturned boats, with no windows, and a door through which one had to crawl. Whole families lived in these dwellings, without furnishings save for floor mats and a stone for a pillow. They cultivated no animals except fowls, and although they grew bananas and sugar cane, the sweet potato or yam was the basic food of the island. They possessed no metal implements and cooked their food over stones glowing in earthen ovens.

They were a friendly people, and the Dutchmen saw no weapons of any kind. Roggeveen noted in his log that they were a happy, polite, peaceful people, but consummate thieves. They even stole hats off the heads of the sailors. In an argument which arose over the stealing of a tablecloth, one native was shot on board and a dozen others ashore. The baffled natives were left with their dead and wounded while the Dutch ship sailed away.

Not until 1769 did another European vessel, the *Saint-Jean-Baptiste*, under the French Captain de Surville of the Pondicherry Company, call at the island. Unfortunately, we have no record of this expedition. The following year, however, a Spanish man-of-war commanded by Don Felipe Gonzales y Haedo and a frigate arrived to take possession of the island in the name of the Spanish king and the Viceroy of Peru. Like the Dutch, they had been attracted by smoke signals sent up by the islanders. They went ashore with two priests and a small party of soldiers, and were taken to the Poike Peninsula (the eastern apex of this triangular island), accompanied by gleeful and dancing natives.

The expeditionary force planted three crosses, sang a few songs, fired a salute, declared the island to be the possession of Spain, and christened it San Carlos Island. Just to keep the proceedings legal, the Spaniards had the natives endorse the formal possession. The islanders could not, of course, read the document, but the boldest of them signed with a Rongo-Rongo character representing a bird (an ideograph in Easter Island writing). This is important, because it suggests that the islanders still knew the art of writing on tablets.

In 1771 and 1772, the Viceroy of Peru sent two other expeditions to map the island in detail. Although both expeditions appear to have been carried out quite diligently, the information they acquired has been lost. The Spaniards did note one item of interest in their logbooks: the tallest of the bearded, fair-skinned islanders measured from six feet to six feet five inches.

Both gifts and stolen items disappeared so quickly that the Spaniards suspected the natives of having underground caves. No children were to be seen, and only a few women. At this time, the whole island was open and treeless.

Two years later, Captain James Cook arrived, but there were few islanders to greet him. Only a few hundred people lived on the island, almost all men; they were under middle height and, by the standards of Cook's men, miserable and indifferent. Noticing the few women and lack of children, Cook correctly surmised that many of the islanders had gone underground, that some great calamity had occurred since the Spaniards' visit. Patrols sent all over the island failed to locate the missing populace, despite the barrenness of the land. Plagued by scurvy, Cook and his men left the island in despair, having traded for yams. But they were cheated: the natives had filled the baskets with stones, with only a few potatoes on top.

Cook noted that during his visit some of the statues were standing and others had collapsed. This important fact gives us an approximate date for the decline of the island's art and religion. Also, once again there was theft, and once again there was gunfire.

Twelve years later, the Comte de La Pérouse anchored his expedition for twenty-four hours off the island. Despite several thefts, La Pérouse, an eighteenth-century gentleman, did not regard the theft of a sailor's hat as an adequate reason for killing a man. He sent ashore pigs, poultry, and other livestock, intended for cultivation on the island, but the natives, plagued by drought and poverty, ate them; his gardener dispensed seeds and plants, some of which survived.

Unlike earlier explorers, La Pérouse found that nearly half the population was composed of mature women, swarms of children—as if all spawned from the bowels of the earth into a volcanic moonscape. They crawled out of their dark retreats, the subterranean passages which Cook's men had not been shown. They had hidden their aristocracy, the women and children, and their most important possessions underground. As Cook before him, La Pérouse noted that the then existing population could have had nothing to do with the ancient statues. It had not even attempted to maintain the foundations of the walled terraces.

From Cook's entries, it was to be understood that the statues were not ordinary images, but memorials to earlier *arikis*, memorials to those of holy and royal birth. Skeletons and bones proved that some form of ancestor worship and a belief in a life after death were prevalent among the early islanders.

Apart from the Russian ship *Neva*, no other vessels visited the island until the American ship *Nancy* in 1805. This New Bedford schooner reached Easter Island with the intention of capturing a dozen hands to hunt seals. In addition, they captured ten women, for obvious purposes. After three days, the shackled prisoners were released and jumped overboard; despite pursuit, none were captured and none were ever seen again.

In 1811 the American whaler *Pindos* pulled in. Its long boats went ashore to bring fresh water, fresh vegetables, and fresh women—not necessarily in that order. After a night of proving their masculinity, the sailors put the girls back into boats and when they were near land, forced them to jump overboard.

On December 12, 1862, six Peruvian ships appeared in Hangaroa Bay. Unsuspectingly, the natives signed a contract, and when they wanted to go ashore, they were chained and bound for slavery in guano quarries of Peru. Eight of the slave hunters placed brightly colored clothes and other gifts upon the shore. When several hundred curious islanders had gathered around, they were seized. Those who attempted to jump over the cliffs into the sea were fired upon.

On that Christmas Eve of 1862, Easter Island lay all but decimated. Those who were not lying dead upon the rocks were either bound upon the ships or had crawled into their catacombs and had rolled stones in front of the openings. Captain Aiguire did not raise anchor until his crew celebrated Christmas.

In May of the following year, the schooner *Favorite* brought six of the natives back; with them came Brother Eugène Eyraud, whose gentleness converted all of the islanders to Christianity. Unfortunately, after his death, the tragic history of this unhappy island continued. In 1870, two years after Brother Eyraud's death, a furious enmity sprang up between two settlers, Captain Dutrou-Bornier and Brother Roussel. Shots were exchanged, and before the matter was settled, many huts had been burned and natives on both sides were killed or wounded.

In September 1888, the Chilean Captain Don Policarpo Toro suddenly arrived to claim the island for his country, to which it still belongs. Despite the sparse vegetation, he very quickly granted the firm of Williamson and Balfour Co. the rights to raise sheep. To this day, the island belongs as much to sheep as it does to people.

The almost comically tragic history of Easter Island has continued well into our own century, hiding its prehistory still more deeply. But in 1914, a remarkable woman, one Miss Katherine S. Routledge, arrived upon her own sailing yacht and mapped and surveyed all that was aboveground. She was so busy with her pioneering efforts that there was no time for excavations. She clearly recognized the mysteries she had left unsolved—and she left their solution to those who would come after her.

In 1934 a Franco-Belgian expedition arrived. The Belgian Lavachery devoted his time to examining thousands of stoneworks and rock carvings. The French scientist Alfred Métraux collected the remaining oral tradition of the natives for a large-scale ethnographic study. He observed: "The island lives in such a degree of wretchedness that it is impossible to speak of transition from a primitive state to our civilization. Easter Island, neglected by the Chileans or disastrously influenced by those men who are sent there, has not fallen into decadence; it has simply rotted in the midst of hopeless destitution."

No excavations were begun until the Thor Heyerdahl expedition of 1955–56, which may have solved some of the mysteries of Easter Island. Heyerdahl's theory, while subject to criticism on many details, remains the only theory with a hard core of fact and the one which must be disproved before another can be put in its place. Earlier scholars claimed that the Easter Island people were descendants of ancient civilizations in India, China, or even Egypt. A wilder theory still is that the red-haired founders of the island were the survivors of the legendary continent of Mu, which was destroyed by a cataclysm similar to that which was supposed to have destroyed Atlantis. More serious historians believe that Easter Islanders were Polynesian colonists who sailed eastward and settled there after stopping at other islands along the way. But, if this is so, why are no examples of Easter Island–style writing or art found in Micronesia or Melanesia?

Heyerdahl maintains people from a pre-Incan culture in Peru (perhaps the Tiahuanacos—certainly the large statues found on Easter Island remind one of the stone "giants" found at Tiahuanaco) floated on reed rafts, following the Humboldt Current, nearly two thousand years ago, and populated the islands of Polynesia. Heyerdahl cites a legend in which ancient "gods" sailed westward into the ocean, a principal legend among the tribes of pre-Columbian America. The Easter Islanders maintain that their ancestors were red-haired people who arrived, about two hundred strong, from the east. Heyerdahl's excavations established a remarkable similarity in art and sculpture between Polynesia and Peru.

According to Heyerdahl's theory, Easter Island had three waves of immigration. Based on the carbon 14 dating of the oldest artifacts on the island, the first wave arrived about 300 A.D., allowing for a hundred-year margin of error either way. These tall, fair-skinned, red-headed people created the stone platforms and small figurines. A second wave came from Peru about 1100, after the first settlers had been decimated by sickness and famine. The second wave of immigrants, also tall and fair-haired, built the large statues and established a peaceful, stable, and sophisticated society based upon agriculture. Finally, a third and different group arrived about 1400. This time the immigrants came from the western Polynesian islands; they were short, stout, dark-skinned people. Despite racial differences, the new arrivals settled peacefully on the island, intermarried, and even helped with the unending project of erecting more statues.

The stones for the statues were quarried from the slope of an old volcano, where numerous half-finished figures have been found. The soft reddish-brown rock was cut into great slabs from the mountainside and carved on the spot. The completed statues were then hauled down the slope on sledges made of reeds. A gang of two hundred men, using a jerky seesaw motion, could easily have moved a twelve-ton stone in this fashion, although progress would have been slow. At the ceremonial site near the coast, the islanders stood the gigantic figures on their terraces. They probably used a technique similar to that used by the builders of Stonehenge, placing small stones under one stone, then wedging dirt beneath it until the larger stone stood upright.

Although carving of the statues appears to have been a part of the religious observation of the "long-ears," the tall, red-headed descendants of the peoples who arrived from Peru, the hauling and erection of the figures was hard, demanding, tedious work which, along with most of the other physical labor, seems to have fallen to the "short-ears," those dark-skinned arrivals from Polynesia. The "long-ear" priests supervised the work.

Finally, the "short-ears" could no longer tolerate the unequal division of labor, and revolted. In the civil war that followed, the "long-ears" were all but exterminated, the statues overthrown, and the old culture destroyed. Thereupon the "short-ears" reverted to barbarism and cannibalism; coupled with family feuds, this state of affairs continued until the time Brother Eyraud arrived in 1863.

We do know that as late as the Cook voyage the "long-ear" civilization remained intact. One of Cook's men made an excellent likeness of a "long-ear," complete with feathered headdress and unmistakable Caucasian features. Local legend places the revolt at about 1780. The island custom of snipping a lock of hair from each generation and of knotting and preserving it enables us to date the rebellion, from the existing "long-ear" descendants, to within ten years of that date.

The "long-ears" were an energetic people with their own system of writing and religion, and intent upon improving the island with walls, roads, and docks—all made of stone. An agricultural people, they decided to rid the island of all superfluous stones, so that all the earth could be cultivated. Work was begun on the Poike Plateau, and the "short-ears" began to carry every single stone and fling it into the sea. To this day, there is not a loose stone on this grassy peninsula, while the rest of this volcanic island is covered with red scree and lava blocks.

Many years before, to prevent theft, the "long-ears" had buried their treasures in the numerous caves on the island. Each family had its own cave. Under the command of their chief, Iko, they dug a trench nearly two miles long, twelve feet deep, and forty feet wide, which separated the Poike peninsula from the rest of the island. This they filled with branches and tree trunks, which they planned to set on fire should the "short-ears" attempt to storm the slope which led up from the plain. On the other three sides of the peninsula was a sheer drop of six hundred feet to the sea.

But one of the "long-ears" had a "short-ear" wife, named Moko Pingei. She arranged for her people to steal past the place where they saw her sitting, weaving a large basket. They saw her plaiting one night at the end of Iko's

155

ditch, stole past, and sneaked around the outer edge of the plateau until they had completely surrounded Poike. Another army of "short-ears" marched openly up the slope. The "long-ears" lined up to face them and set fire to the whole pyre. At this point, the "short-ears" rushed forward from their hiding places, and in the bloody fighting which followed, all the "long-ears" were either killed or driven back into their own burning ditch.

Three of the "long-ears" escaped by leaping through the fire and hiding in a cave. One, the progenitor of "long-ear" descendants, was called Ororoina, another Vai, and the name of the third the "short-ears" no longer remember. They were found, and two of them were stabbed to death. The third was allowed to remain alive, perhaps as a relic or as a precautionary propriation to the "long-ear" gods. His remembered name may very well not have been his name. When he was dragged from the cave, he was crying *"Orro, orro, orro"* in his own tongue, but it was a language which the "short-ears," despite their centuries on the island, did not understand.

Alfred Métraux in his *Ethnology of Easter Island* (reprinted in Honolulu in 1940), along with Mrs. Routledge and other early explorers, concluded that the legend was an invention of fairly recent times. What remains a fact, however, is that for nearly a hundred years the "short-ears" reverted to the barbarism they had probably known before they came to the island. They preferred human flesh to either fish or poultry; cannibalism ravaged the island, and the "short-ears" took refuge in deep, narrow caves where a family might defend itself from its neighbors. All civilization was lost, except for what the descendants of Ororoina preserved, including the written language of the *rongo-rongo*, which, however, they largely lost the ability to read.

Does the mystery of the red-haired "gods" of the Incas end with the massacre on Easter Island? Perhaps not. Stone constructions, otherwise unknown in Polynesia, may also be found on a relatively direct route from Easter Island, along the Humboldt Current in Eastern Polynesia: in human form on Pitcairn Island (1,100 miles from Easter Island); stone cities on Rapa Iti (about 270 miles from

Pitcairn); and large stone statues in human form at Raivavae (360 miles north of Rapa Iti) and on Nuku Hiva and Fatu Hiva (about 900 miles northeast of Tahiti).

When Captain Bligh's mutinous crew from the HMS *Bounty* arrived on Pitcairn in 1790, the island was uninhabited. They found abandoned temple platforms with skulls and a few small statues which faintly recalled the giants on Easter Island. No archaeologist has spent more than a few hours on the island. The descendants of the *Bounty* crews leveled the temple platforms to the ground and smashed the small red statues and threw them into the sea.

The only evidence that there may once have been an Easter Island culture on Mangareva is a statue of a French missionary, his foot upon a broken heathen idol. However, the legend of King Tupa may suggest further evidence. According to the natives, however, the legendary King Tupa came to the island from the east with numerous rafts with masts and sails, each large enough to carry a hundred or more people.

After staying several months, King Tupa returned to his eastern kingdom and was never seen by the Mangarevians again. Thor Heyerdahl speculates in *Aku-Aku*, "In time and place this legend tallies astonishingly well with the Incas' legend of their own great ruler Tupac, who caused an immense flotilla of balsa sailing rafts to be built and set out to visit distant inhabited islands he had heard of from his own seafaring merchants. According to Inca historians, Tupac spent almost a year on his cruise in the open Pacific, and returned to Peru with prisoners and booty after visiting two inhabited islands. I know now, thanks to the experiments we had carried out subsequent to the Kon-Tiki expedition, that such a raft cruise is entirely feasible, as we had finally rediscovered the lost Inca art of navigating a balsa raft with their *guara* or centerboard method. This enabled a raft to work to windward just as readily as any sailing boat. And Inca Tupac may well have been the Tupa remembered at Mangareva."

On Rapa Iti, which lies to the southwest of Mangareva, are mountains topped with what appear to be Aztec pyramids overgrown with foliage, or the stepped fortresses of the Incas. The first European to view the crest of the mountain chain, Morongo Uta, was Captain George Vancouver in 1791. He observed people running about on the structure and presumed it was a man-made fort. He never went ashore. As late as 1932, Eugène Caillot, in his *Histoire de l'Ile Oparo ou Rapa*, who had climbed into the hills and observed masonry protruding from the overgrowth, regarded the formations as long-forgotten forts, although others thought them to be agricultural terraces.

The Heyerdahl excavations of 1956 revealed the structure to be not a single building but the ruins of a whole village. The early natives, instead of settling in the fertile valleys, had climbed to the most inaccessible peaks and carved their villages out of the mountain rock. Around and below Morongo Uta, great terraces with houses in rows were carved out of the cliffs. Curious stone ovens, full of charcoal and ashes, were of a type found only on Easter Island and nowhere else in Polynesia. Stone adzes were found in great abundance, as were *popoi* pounders, which the women had used to grind food. The tools were so perfectly polished, formed, and balanced that it was difficult for the explorers to believe that they could have been made without the use of the modern lathe.

Heyerdahl writes: "A huge moat with a rampart on the raised village side barred the way to anyone coming along the southern ridge. Hundreds of thousands of hard basalt stones had been painfully carried up from the bottom of the valley to support the terraces on which the huts rested. . . . The uncut blocks were fitted together in a masterly fashion without mortar; here and there a drainage channel ran out through the wall, or long stones projected and formed a kind of stair from one terrace to the next."

Morongo Uta is the largest continuous structure in the whole of Polynesia and the only one built of stone. It is 160 feet high with a span of 1,300 feet, and its over eighty terraces housed more people than live on the island today, some 278. The dwellings themselves were made with boughs stuck into the earth, bent into an oval and bound on top, then covered with reeds and dried grass, like a mound of hay. These dwellings are reminiscent of those found on Easter Island. Equally conspicuous is the lack of temples, which are found throughout Polynesia. On this point Heyerdahl notes: "The population of Morongo Uta had solved this problem in a manner so far unknown in the whole Pacific; they had cut small dome-shaped niches in the rock behind the terraces, and there they had built themselves miniature temples, on whose flat floors rows and squares of small stone prisms stood on edge like chessmen. Such ceremonies as could not be performed in front of these pocket-size temples could be carried out on the topmost platform of the pyramid. . . ."

Who were these strange stone builders, and what had so frightened them that they built their villages only on the mountaintops of Rapa Iti? According to the natives, in a legend written down about a hundred years ago, the island was first settled by women who arrived from Easter Island. Many of them were pregnant, and it is from their offspring that the population of the island was formed. Like most legends, this one doubtless contains an element of fact, if one can decipher the legend. Pregnant women did not build the stone villages of Rapa Iti, nor could they populate them with as many people as were seen by Captain Vancouver in 1791, not if they were survivors of the Easter Island massacre.

These Pacific hillmen did not build their stone villages because they were frightened of one another. All the houses of the villages were built in a continuous line along the ridges, forming a defense system that looked out upon the ocean. It would appear that they were afraid of an enemy known to them, and who would come to them from the sea. Perhaps it was an enemy who had already driven them from another island. Could the legend of the Rapa Iti natives, the legend that they had come from Easter Island, be true? If so, then we must suppose an earlier incident in the history of that troubled island than the great massacre of 1780–90.

Although none of the great stone statues of the type to be found on Easter Island exist on Rapa Iti, this fact may be due to the lack of space and a fear of mounting them on the shore, where they might attract ancient enemies.

Human figures carved in stone, however, are to be found. In a bluff high above the valley to the east of Morongo Uta, a rock chamber was cut into the cliff. Here they buried their kings. Shaped like a large sarcophagus and cut in profile, the open side has been artfully concealed. In a cliff beside it is a child-sized human figure cut in relief.

At this place, according to tradition, kings were laid to rest with great pomp and in broad daylight, their heads pointing east. Shortly thereafter, during the night, they were secretly carried away over the ridge to the Anarua Valley, probably by priests, who alone knew the location of the true burial chamber: a cave behind a thirty-foot waterfall. Inside the cave lies a subterranean lake, with burial cairns along its shores.

To the north, in the Marquesa group, lie the islands of Nuku Hiva and Hiva Oa. On the former island lies the famous Taipi Valley of which Herman Melville wrote. Around a ruined temple in the Valley are eleven red stone human-shaped figures. Carbon 14 datings reveal that the oldest of them were carved about 1300, or 900 years after man had first settled on Easter Island. In the Puamao Valley of Hiva Oa, there is another group of stone figures, the largest of which measures only eight feet.

Both carbon dating and the statuary itself suggest that the mother culture of these stone-carving islanders lay upon Easter Island. Numerous collateral reasons support this conclusion. If we suppose that the stone culture of Polynesia moved from west to east, from Asia toward South America, we encounter the difficulty of why the Dutch, at a relatively late period and with relatively sophisticated ships, could not navigate against the prevailing winds and tides; why nearly all discoveries of the South Pacific islands have been made by ships sailing from east to west.

Further: so far, no carbon datings have placed any Polynesian culture earlier than 800 A.D., and traditional Pacific scholars agree that the islands remained uninhabited until about 500 A.D. If all migrations had been from Asia, then Easter Island could not have been settled until about 1400, about the time when Polynesian people do appear to have reached the island. Some scholars date their arrival as late as 1500 or 1600, not long before the

Europeans arrived in 1722. The evidence of the island does not support such a conclusion, for we know that by 280 to 480 highly organized human labor existed.

The tightly fitted, unmortared masonry of Easter Island is unlike anything to be found in the more westward islands. But, far from being the most recent achievement of the South Sea islanders, as earlier archaeologists supposed, it is the achievement of the earliest settlers and typically Peruvian in its style. The apparent uniformity and originality of the local style, shown in the famous heads of the almost-buried statues, is also revealing. Excavations have established the existence of diverse styles, the earliest of which are similar to pre-Incan statues of Tiahuanaco, Peru. The better-known busts and heads were the products of the second migration. The first settlers had introduced masonry work and the more diversified styles which were the prototypes of the Easter Island statues.

Carbon datings of the two great stone groups in the Marquesas, those of Hive Oa and Nuku Hiva, were erected about 1300 and 1500, respectively. By such a late date, the red-haired Easter Islanders might well have spread their culture to the warlike natives of Hiva Oa, who later, in the third migration to Easter Island, might have repaid their visit. Otherwise, the evidence remains that the stone culture characteristic of Peru spread to the easternmost islands of Polynesia in a chronological sequence.

Excavations at the "oven of the long-ears" established that a natural depression was transformed into a defensive position about 400 A.D. Nothing indicates a war earlier than the massacre of 1780–90. But like the people of Rapa Iti, the first settlers of Easter Island were a cautious people. Carbon 14 tests indicate that an enormous fire was ignited in the trench about 1670. Thor Heyerdahl wrote in 1956, "Native tradition insists that this pyre was lighted eleven generations ago. Pacific scholars reckon an average of twenty-five years to a Polynesian generation, which would bring us back to about 1680, only a decade off our own carbon date."

Peruvian yams or sweet potatoes, gourds, and species of cotton are known to have been transported from island to island in southeastern Polynesia by pre-European voyagers. The *totora* reed, which grows in the crater lakes of Easter Island, also comes from Peru and was the primary building material for the houses and boats of the earliest islanders.

Still further, discoveries have revealed that the architects of the first migrations were sun worshipers who made solstice observations and structured their religious observances accordingly. More important, blood samples prove conclusively that a direct infusion from Malaya to Polynesia, despite slight linguistic similarities, is unlikely. Blood analysis shows that even the present population of Easter Island conforms markedly to samples of North and South American Indians and differs considerably from those of Indonesians, Malays, Micronesians, and Melanesians, as well as other Southeast Asian peoples.

However, although we have solved many of the mysteries of Easter Island through recent excavations, the basic mystery remains: Who were the red-haired strangers who first came to the island? Even Heyerdahl's interesting, and largely proven, explanation remains only a theory.

The true secret of the great stone faces of Easter Island may be hidden on one of the *rongo-rongo* or "talking boards." These highly polished slabs of wood are covered with intricately carved ideographs, which represent the island's ancient language.

Unfortunately, no one living today can read this lost language with any ease. Linguistic experts have so far been unable to decipher the writing. All but a handful of *rongo-rongos* were destroyed by Christian missionaries of the 1800s. Still, more and more of the ancient "talking boards" are being found in secret caves of Easter Island, and archaeologists still hope that one of them will eventually reveal the real story of Easter Island.

City of the Dead

Neil Richards

We know a great deal about ancient Egypt, Greece, and Rome, because we are able to study the written records of these civilizations and have learned to analyze the findings of archaeologists. But Tiahuanaco, the "City of the Dead" in the high mountains of Bolivia, has never been examined with the tools of modern scholarship. The ruins of Tiahuanaco may be 5,000 years old, or 10,000, or even 20,000. Massive stonework, giant monoliths, strange statues with cryptic carvings are silent witnesses to a civilization that seems to have dropped out of history. Mr. Richards engaged in excavations during a two-year tour of duty with the U.S. Army Mission in La Paz, capital of Bolivia.

Archaeologists have known for a long time that the ancient cultures of Peru and Bolivia date back to periods long before the rise of the Incas and that these earlier cultures were distinctly different from that of the Incas. Perhaps it is only because the Incas ruled the last great native empire in South America that their civilization has captured the imaginations and attention of most modern-day researchers and historians. Yet the earlier cultures may have an importance in the history of man unequaled by any other ancient race.

One such ancient culture flourished in the "City of the Dead," Tiahuanaco, where the chill winds of the Bolivian *altiplano* (high plateau) sweep across Lake Titicaca today as they have for uncounted centuries. The ruins left by this unknown civilization are almost forgotten, although evidence indicates Tiahuanaco once may have dominated an area greater than the Inca empire ruled at its height. Of the builders of this city only their works—massive stonework, giant monoliths, strange statues with cryptic carving—remain standing on the barren plateau in mute testimony that once men lived, loved, ruled, and died here.

From Quechua, the language of the Incas, comes the name Tiahuanaco, meaning "City of the Dead." And we know from sources other than this descriptive name that the city was already in ruins when the legions of the expanding empire began to march southward in the thirteenth century. Even then local tribes apparently offered no explanation for the city to their new rulers. Not being an inquisitive people the Incas were content to accept the city as the burial place of an ancient race and to ignore it.

In 1533 Francisco Pizarro's conquistadores were interested only in gold. After this small band of adventurers murdered Atahuallpa and destroyed the spirit of the empire, they concerned themselves with acquiring gold as fast as possible and, finding that Tiahuanaco apparently offered no treasure, they too accepted the ruins as merely another mystery of the new world.

As late as the nineteenth century numerous monoliths still stood among the ruins. Now, although many of these are displayed in collections around the world, only one remains in its original position. For centuries Indians of the region have used the ruins as a quarry, constructing their dwellings of carved stone taken from there. More recently, during the building of Bolivia's single railroad, irreplaceable statuary and stonework were ground up to make the railroad bed. A few small archaeological expeditions have excavated at the site, but their efforts have been unscientific and ineffectual. No major scientific attempt to study the city ever has been made.

Wendell Bennett's 1932 expedition unearthed evidence indicating that the city is at least 5,000 years old. He also discovered the largest Tiahuanaco monolith ever found, along with artifacts so sophisticated there can be no doubt that the inhabitants of this city were as highly advanced as any ancient people known to modern man.

Unfortunately these discoveries were not followed by careful study. Today the ruins of this once mighty city still stand as an unexplained mystery, visited by llama herders and only occasionally by modern men.

The first man to recognize the significance of Tiahuanaco as a pre-Columbian culture of major importance was Arthur Posnansky, a German archaeologist. He was so impressed by the city that he became a Bolivian citizen and devoted nearly fifty years to archaeological research on this spot. Although hampered by lack of modern facilities, political obstacles and local ignorance, his studies convinced him that the city was older than anything on the South American continent, perhaps 10,000 to 20,000 years old! He traced pottery and other artifacts distinctly Tiahuanacan in design to locations as far north as the northern coastal deserts of Peru and as far south as Argentina. He became convinced that the culture had had a hitherto unsuspected influence over a vast region of the South American highlands.

Posnansky believed the *altiplano* was once much closer to sea level than its present 13,000 or more feet. The geological features of the region indicate both that the climate was once semitropical and that Lake Titicaca has changed in size and depth. Gigantic upheavals in comparatively recent geological time apparently caused the whole region to rise, probably in a terrible cataclysm.

These changes in the earth's crust did not destroy the city but undoubtedly made it a less desirable place to live. Posnansky was intrigued by the fact that the city does not show signs of forced evacuation. In other words, neither war nor natural disaster seem to be direct causes for the disappearance of the builders. He believed his data showed that the mysterious citizens left voluntarily.

Because the city was abandoned rather than destroyed, little evidence exists with which to reconstruct the daily life of the inhabitants. Posnansky hoped that the men who were capable of such tremendous and sophisticated work would have left some message for posterity—if only modern man could uncover it. But just when he thought he was close to the solution in 1946, Arthur Posnansky died—before he could unravel the mystery.

One interesting fact cited by Posnansky to support his theories is that the present-day Indians of the region display neither the physical nor artistic characteristics of the builders of the city. The pottery and artwork found in the ruins indicate a taller people with distinctive facial characteristics seemingly unrelated to the prominent cheekbones of today's inhabitants of the high plateau.

The differences between Tiahuanaco and pre-Columbian and modern cultures are significant and interesting. However, the really startling facts are its similarities with other ancient cultures, particularly Egyptian.

Within the ruins is a structure known locally as the *Calassassayax* (house of worship). It appears to be a raised temple surrounded by upright stones, like columns. These stones are fitted and joined by a method not used by the Incas or their immediate predecessors. The joints and facing parts were polished to make a nearly perfect match. The only other ancient people known to polish their stonework were the Egyptians.

Though on a smaller scale, the design and layout of this structure is similar to Karnak; in fact, the relative dimensions of the *Calassassayax* make it in many ways a scale model of that famous Egyptian temple. The distances between the columns and the length and width are approximately one-fifth the dimensions of Karnak.

A huge earth mound dominates the Tiahuanaco ruins. It is now so eroded and worn that its purpose is not clear. Apparently it once was faced with distinctive green stones. From the method of paving and the fact that the stones are not native to the area, observers have concluded that its construction must have been carefully planned. Roughly measured dimensions indicate the mound was square at the base. A great depression in the center with some foundation stones still in place has led some observers to conclude the mound was a reservoir. Another theory, however, points to what may have been a purposeful conjunction of the mound with the temple and suggests that the mound may have been hollow. It also is possible the mound was a pyramid. It seems unlikely that extensive carving would be done on stones intended to line a reservoir.

Other unique features are to be found in the ruins. There is a massive grandstand carved out of one solid piece of andesite weighing a hundred tons. Huge finished stones weighing many tons were placed in such a way that only a people with advanced engineering knowledge could have designed them, let alone moved them. The andesite used in this construction was quarried at some unknown spot. The builders' quarry never has been found; the closest possible place is fifty miles away in the mountains.

The Tiahuanacans used a peculiar T-slot device to join some of their decorative stonework. These slots were carved carefully into the stone much as a carpenter chisels places for hinges. The finished slots presumably were filled with copper or gold. In their decorative stonework the Tiahuanacans displayed artistic refinement not usually seen in South America. Intricate designs in relief can be seen on everything connected with the ruins. The so-called "sun gate" shows exceptionally fine work. This piece is a stone archway carved from a single block of andesite and covered by an interconnecting detailed carving. The central feature is a head which may depict the sun-god. It has been suggested that this carving actually is a message, engraved in stone. There are some similarities to cuneiform writing but if this is so no one has been able to decipher them. The particular carvings used are unique to Tiahuanaco and have not been found anywhere else in the world.

Certain pictures and drawings in the ruins depict reed boats used on Lake Titicaca by the builders. These carefully woven boats, still used today, are indeed one of the distinctive points of tourist interest in the lake region. And these boats could have come from an Egyptian museum; their method of construction and dimensions are identical to the type of boat used on the Nile since before the time of Moses.

Some modern authorities believe these boats are examples of "cultural coincidence." They point out that the reeds used are similar to the reeds along the banks of the Nile and that it is only logical to assume that given the same materials, two widely separated cultures may produce identical artifacts.

This suggestion of cultural coincidence might be accepted for reed boats, but it becomes utterly fantastic when applied to medical instruments.

The ancient Tiahuanacans practiced the art of trepanning or opening the brain. Clubs, spears, and hand-thrown missiles caused frequent head injuries which probably often developed into tumors. The Tiahuanacans practiced a method of opening the skull to relieve pressure or remove growths. Some artifacts taken from the ruins are small statuettes that show both the injury and the operation. That some of these operations were successful is proved by well-preserved skulls found in the ruins. Well-healed bone grafts testify that the ancient doctors were highly skilled, with a surprising knowledge of anatomy.

The most startling facts about these operations, however, are the surgical instruments. The Tiahuanacan's copper trepanning instruments are *identical* to those used by the Egyptians, one of the very few ancient races to practice this same method of treatment. The credibility of "cultural coincidence" is stretched considerably when related to brain operations. It is possible to accept the fact that two cultures may have developed a form of brain operation (although few did), but that both cultures used identical instruments and methods seems unusual to say the least. The instruments are of a high grade of copper and include drills and chisels. In themselves they indicate an advanced degree of metallurgy, knowledge of simple machinery, and development of surgical practices far more detailed than can be expected in primitive societies.

The science of trepanning was practiced by later cultures in South America, notably the Incas, but the fact that the procedure was known so much earlier is a mystery frankly unexplained.

Some persons in South America have an intense interest in the ruins of Tiahuanaco. They believe that Posnansky was close to a complete answer and that his theories are supported by sound evidence. Later authorities conveniently have ignored Posnansky and his work.

The cultural similarities between Egypt and Tiahuanaco strongly suggest there must have been contact between the two.

Is it possible then that civilization was born in the New World and spread to Egypt as a result of geological changes in the land mass of South America?

Or was some forgotten Egyptian explorer blown off his course and forced to found a new civilization and live out an exile thousands of miles from home?

How did a technically sophisticated empire rise and fall in one of the most remote and forbidding regions in the world? Who were the engineers who built a city of stone on the barren *altiplano*? When and from where did they come? Where did they go?

Whatever the answers—for that matter, whatever the questions—no one has offered a convincing explanation for these ruins, ruins which are so different from those found in other parts of South America, ruins that alone and mutely testify to an empire whose bounds only can be surmised and whose inhabitants are lost in time.

The Restless Coffins of Barbados

Iris M. Owen

What happens when a modern investigator comes across a well-established, eerie legend? The case of the moving coffins on the Caribbean island of Barbados provides an answer to this question. Mrs. Owen, secretary of the New Horizons Research Foundation, Toronto, became aware that most accounts of the mysteriously mobile coffins were "a rehash of previous accounts, incorporating the writers' own theories and prejudices." Reports of the moving coffins date from the nineteenth century, and Mrs. Owen says, "I could find no accounts of recent visits to the vault, in spite of the influx of modern tourism to the island." Together with her husband, Prof. A.R.G. Owen, Department of Mathematics, University of Toronto, Iris Owen paid two visits to the vaults, because, as she put it, "I felt that some modern observations might not be amiss."

For those unfamiliar with the story the details briefly are these. In the churchyard of Christ Church in Barbados there is a family vault, belonging to a family named Chase, local plantation owners and a white family, resident in Barbados. The vault was opened in 1807, when the body of a Mrs. Goddard was placed in it. In 1808 Miss A. M. Chase was interred there, and in 1812 Miss D.

Chase was also buried in the vault. When later in 1812 the vault was again opened to receive the body of the Honorable T. Chase the three previous coffins had apparently been moved around and were in some disarray. On Sept. 25, 1816, an infant child was to be buried, and again, on opening the vault, the four coffins (which had been rearranged tidily when the Hon. T. Chase was buried) were found to have been moved and disturbed. Two months later, when the vault was opened to receive the body of a Mr. Brewster, and again in 1819, when a Mr. Clarke was buried, the coffins were found to be disarranged. Each time they were replaced in their original positions, and the vault sealed between each opening. The door was a massive cement slab, requiring six or seven men to move it, and it was cemented in place. The floor of the vault was sand, and no footmarks or disturbance of the sand was apparent after each opening. The coffins were originally three on the floor side by side, and the others laid on top of them. Most of the coffins were of lead, but there seems some doubt about Mrs. Goddard's, which may have been of wood.

As would be expected, these mysterious happenings caused a great deal of interest and speculation, not to say dismay, and when in July 1819 a Mrs. Thomasina Clarke was due to be buried (this time in a wooden coffin), the Governor of Barbados himself, Lord Combermere, together with his aide-de-camp, and a large crowd of interested and excited spectators, decided to be present at the opening of the vault. Again the coffins were found to be in great disorder. The interior of the vault was carefully examined, and no trace could be found of any secret entrance. The coffins were replaced, the floor carefully covered with sand (presumably in order that any footprints of possible intruders would show), and the cement slab replaced and carefully sealed. The governor himself put his own seal on it, and various other people present also added their own marks. The largest coffin had been placed on the ground, and the others placed on top. Some accounts say the children's coffins, of which there were three, were placed on bricks in the vault, but whatever the arrangement, the vault was getting crowded. The only wooden coffin (apart from the one just placed inside), that of Mrs. Goddard, had practically fallen to pieces during the various disturbances, and was tied in a bundle, according to contemporary accounts, and stacked against the wall.

In April 1820, eight months after the last burial, after hearing rumors that noises had been heard in the vinicity of the vault, the governor ordered the vault reopened, although there was no body to be interred—the motive seems to have been curiosity. The governor, the rector, and two or three other persons of eminence, together with an excited crowd that is reported to have numbered thousands, were present at this opening. The governor's seal and the other private marks were found to be untouched, completely as they had been left, and undisturbed. But, once again, the coffins themselves were in a state of utter confusion. One was standing on end, against the door itself, rendering it difficult to open the vault. The remains of the wooden coffin were still stacked against the wall. At this stage the governor gave permission for the bodies to be removed and buried elsewhere, and for the vault to be left empty.

Controversy over what actually happened has raged intermittently even since, and obviously at this late date any kind of proof of what occurred is out of the question. Nevertheless, when one actually visits the site, as opposed to reading about it, one or two points strike one with some degree of force, and perhaps should be added to the general account.

The vault is a minor tourist attraction in Barbados today, to the extent only that the details of the above story, as related, appear on a notice posted in the church porch, and over the vault itself. A copy of a contemporary account is currently out of print, due (we were told) to lack of interest.

The churchyard is, as has been said, on the top of a hill, some 250 feet above sea level, and a mile or so from the coast itself—there is a beautiful view over the Caribbean from the churchyard. The main road runs round the brow of the hill, and a small road at a right angle to it leads up to the church itself. There is an open space outside the church wall, and on the opposite side of this a modern school. At the time of the happenings one would imagine this was occupied by the houses of some of the local people. A sturdy wall runs around the churchyard. The Chase vault backs almost onto the church wall—there is approximately fifteen inches of space between the back of the vault and the surrounding church wall. The Chase vault is the only vault along this wall. There is another, much more modern vault, farther down by this wall, but it stands parallel to the wall and is some four feet inside the wall. The rest of the churchyard is full of vaults, all much of the same pattern as the Chase vault, but many more grand and much larger. Burials in vaults continue to take place to this present day, and have apparently continued throughout the two centuries. However, in that churchyard, the only vault that is almost backed onto the surrounding wall is the Chase vault.

The vault itself is half above ground and half below, not completely below ground level, as might have been imagined from some accounts. This is typical of the other vaults in the area. Some accounts say that the vault was dug out of solid limestone rock, but there was, or rather is, certainly a good layer of earth on top today. The "lid" of the vault is a chunk of solid rock, or rather several chunks cemented together. Inside the vault, the floor space is twelve feet long by six and a half feet broad. From inside it is arched, although on the outside it appears square. The sides and overhead arch are made of bricks, with somewhat crumbling mortar between them, although, even today, they appear fairly solid. However, the back of the vault, that which is against the outside churchyard wall, is composed of what seems to be rubble masonry, that is, uneven and random slabs of rubble loosely cemented together, and, today, broken and fallen out in places. At the top of the back portion of the vault the masonry has completely fallen out in a couple of places, and an old, very rusty length of piping can be seen to traverse the whole width of the vault, some four or five inches behind the facing, and between it and the church wall itself. This piping is about six inches below the surface of the ground outside. It looks indeed as if this pipe could have been there for the whole time of the existence of the vault—in fact, it seems unlikely that the earth so near the vault would have been disturbed to lay such a pipe later. We could get no information from local people on this; in fact most people we talked to did not seem to have either noticed it or appreciated its possible significance.

It may be true that there were no signs of water entering the vault at the time of the disturbances; the same is not so today. There are very obvious, and many, stream marks down the back of the vault, apparently emanating from the area of this pipe. The lower part of the vault is obviously damp, and green with fungus. If the pipe did exist at the relevant times, then it is obvious that either through a leak in the pipe itself, or by means of water flowing alongside the pipe, water could have got into the vault, perhaps in large volume at times of heavy storms. This is a hurricane area, and in fact the church was destroyed by a hurricane some eleven years after the happenings. It was rebuilt, and destroyed by fire in 1935, and the present church is the third on the site.

Two points struck us when actually looking at the vault and its surroundings. Firstly, as stated above, the real possibility that water did enter the vault, and float the coffins into their disturbed positions. It has been well established that if lead coffins are properly sealed they will indeed float, as witness the account of the floating coffin of the actor Charles Coghlan in September 1900. Coghlan died in Galveston, Texas, in late 1899, and was buried in a lead-lined coffin in the cemetery there. However, in September 1900 a hurricane struck Galveston and among the damage wrought was the flooding of cemeteries, and the disinterment of bodies by the flood water. Coghlan's coffin was one of those unearthed, and it floated out to sea, making its way by degrees and over a period of time to the shores of Prince Edward Island in Canada, to his own home village, where it was found by local fishermen. The coffin was rescued and reburied in Coghlan's home village with the proper ceremony. (I am indebted to Vincent Gaddis' account of this in his fascinating book *Invisible Horizons — True Mysteries of the Sea*). Rupert Gould, in his book *Oddities*, gives a similar account of a coffin having been picked up off the North Foreland in May 1751, which when opened, contained the body of a man, embalmed and dressed in fine linen, which had been consigned to the Goodwin sands a couple of months previously. So, if water could have got into the Chase vault in large quantities, it is quite possible this could have been the cause of the movements of the coffins. And the vault at the present time certainly does not seem to be waterproof; it is in fact one of the more poorly constructed in a churchyard full of fine vaults.

The other point that seemed to us to offer a possible explanation for the occurrences is the position of the vault itself. As stated previously the vault is very close to the main wall of the churchyard, and in fact is the only one where the back of the vault lies alongside the outer wall. While the present-day wall is very sturdy, being apparently of stone slabs, or bricks, covered over with cement, which would certainly show signs of tampering, there is no record of the old wall that I can find. There would have been a wall, certainly, as it enclosed consecrated ground, but this could have been of bricks only. It appears quite possible that anyone bent on disturbing the vault could more easily enter the vault from the back, rather than try to force an entrance from the front, within the churchyard. It could have been a comparatively easy matter to remove bricks from the churchyard wall, dig out a few inches of earth, and then break into the rough rubble at the back of the vault. It is reported that the Hon. T. Chase was a cruel and unfeeling man. He may have been a hard taskmaster to his slaves—one has to remember that the island was owned by white settlers from Britain, many of whom spent only half their time in the island at sugarcane-cutting time, and the work was done by Negro slaves who were kidnapped in Africa and brought over to the island to do the manual hard labor. The churchyard is off the main road even today, and at nighttime it must be very quiet, and one could work undisturbed. At the time of the happenings it would have been quiet and dark indeed. It could have been an act of revenge, in an effort to frighten away a cruel and unfeeling master; it could equally have been a straightforward attempt at grave robbery, in the hope that valuables had been buried with their owners, but I personally favor the former view. When one walks around the churchyard and reads the history of the time as written on the vaults, one gets a feeling for the period and its history. My own personal feeling is that the vault was entered from the back from motives of revenge at ill treatment. The matter of the undisturbed sand floor is easily explained—nothing would be simpler than to spread fresh sand behind on leaving!

At this late date, one can only speculate. I found it an interesting experience to visit a site about which I had read so many times, and to realize once again that there is nothing like seeing with one's own eyes; imagination can let one down. From the various accounts I have read over the years I had never realized that the vault was placed exactly in the position that it is; neither had I quite appreciated the life and customs of the day, and the situation of the slaves in the society of the island at the time.

Abominable Snowman: Legend or Reality?

William Donehue

Whatever is far away seems exotic. To a Frenchman, events in Tibet and California have almost equally remote charm. But surely to everyone in the civilized world, the high mountains of the snow-covered Himalayas are as exotic and legendary as any one place on earth. Small wonder, then, that reports by explorers and mountaineers from this region continue to cause wonder and awe. Among reports that periodically make news of still higher, more extended, and even more daring Himalayan expeditions, rumors of the discovery of unknown mysterious creatures hold first place. The reality or legend of the Abominable Snowman is examined by Mr. Donehue in detail. The result is an up-to-date and quite definitive account.

There were footprints in the snow, far away from any human settlements, high up on Mount Everest. At a height of 21,000 feet, the pioneer expedition directed by Lieutenant Colonel C.K. Howard-Bury in 1921 came across these strange marks only 1,000 feet below the expedition's highest point, where it discovered a pass, Lhakpa La, leading to the East Rongbuk glacier.

The seemingly human or superhuman footprints were nearly forgotten in the hurly-burly of the expedition's difficulties. It had taken more than a year to make arrangements for the expedition, as the British team of mountaineers needed the cooperation of the Tibetan government. Then one of the expedition's most experienced explorers, A.M. Kellas, died of heart failure because of the physical and psychological stresses.

The mountain, highest peak of the Himalayas, had long been elusive and mysterious. But the footprints were noted and remembered by the expedition's Sherpa porters, who attributed the tracks to the Metch-Kangmi. Literally, *me* means "man" and *kang* means "snow." European travelers called the Snowman "Abominable," partly because of the horror with which the Sherpas, a Himalayan people, regarded the creature, and partly because they mistranslated "Metch" to imply "revolting" or "abominable." Thus, even his name was born in confusion, and in confusion he has remained ever since.

Much has already been written, and still more will be written, of this mysterious creature. Despite numerous investigations, the way of life, and even the existence, of this man-animal remains an enigma. Who or what is the yeti? There is no concrete, undisputed answer. Every suggestion has been put forward from self-hypnosis to the existence of a prehistoric primate.

In earliest times, people were inclined to believe in something mysterious, even when they could find plausible explanations. In our more prosaic age, in which there seems so little left to discover about the world in which we live—with the exception of the conquest of outer space, where we let our imaginations run wild—we remain stubbornly disbelieving in everything which defies a rational explanation. When the Snowman is subjected to the mythic imagination, he appears to us as completely unreal, and, although our imaginations are stirred by the fantasy, we are not able to accept the Snowman as fact.

While a certain amount of imagination is desirable, we should not lose our discernment or critical sense; we should be willing to examine, systematically, everything which is beyond our understanding. In the face of the unknown, detachment is more important than skepticism.

However, even the most impartial investigator of the

Snowman must admit to a basic problem: the great discrepancies in the descriptions of this creature. It has been identified as having the attributes of an ape, on the one hand, and of a bear, on the other. In most cases, these different but abundant descriptions are in accord with the country of their origin. It is natural that people should interpret what they see in accordance with their culture, and the great variation in the legends and traditions of the Snowman are not a *prima facie* proof against its existence.

Discrepancies, however, are not the only difficulty in the evidence regarding the Snowman. As always in matters of this sort, the more reliable witnesses are unwilling to give their names for fear of being laughed at; others do not come forth with their evidence at all. Still another problem is malobservation by even the most sincere and honest of witnesses. We cannot disregard the hypothesis that hermits and other mystics of the Himalayas are at times, at elevated heights, erroneously taken for the Snowman.

There is still another factor present which is difficult to determine and interpret. At these high altitudes, atmospheric conditions produce effects in people which can only be described as hallucinations. However, knowing that a hallucination is possible does not mean that it has occurred in a specific case. The fact that these immaterial visions occur should not cause us to reject all eyewitness evidence.

Superstition and hoaxes have also played their role in the alleged evidence for the Snowman, but a considerable amount of provocative evidence for the Snowman remains. Repetitive and conflicting as the reports sometimes are, we must ask ourselves, is there a prehuman creature? Perhaps a possible answer to our question, "From where did we come?"

Reaction to the evidence for the Snowman, on the part of zoologists and anthropologists, is one of suspicion. They reject any manifestation if it is not the result of an effective analysis based upon skeletal remains. And this condition has never been truly met, despite all the talk about gigantic bones being found in various places, including a deep cave in the Kamloops valley.

There is a very natural spirit of prevention among the

experts; they do not want to be compromised by their own opinions, and they are only slightly interested in any person who has not undertaken serious and trained investigation. Unfortunately, in the mystery of the Abominable Snowman, the evidence is largely based upon expeditions whose primary purpose was mountain climbing, from people who were neither properly equipped nor trained, nor exclusively dedicated to investigating the case. To worsen matters, much of the evidence has been presented by casual observations in letters and by the informality of interviews.

From the very nature of the evidence, many theories would be put forth, for each of which there would be some positive evidence. In the absence of a highly expensive, in-depth investigation by specialists, we must be content to consider the sometimes absurd ideas which have been put forth to explain the mystery of the Snowman. Of all these ideas, perhaps the most meretricious is the "Monkey Theory."

Of the Asiatic monkeys which exist in the Himalayas the most numerous are the langurs (long-tailed), of the genus *Pithecus,* which may be found from Kashmir to the frontier of China, as well as throughout India, Burma, Siam, and the Malay Peninsula, and on coastal islands.

The flat-nosed monkey, of the genus *Rinopithecus,* as well as the Hylobatidae and Simiides species (or in common terms, the gibbon and the anthropoid), are frequently put forward as contenders for being the Snowman. However, they are so strikingly marked, it is difficult to imagine their being confused with other creatures.

Of all the oriental simians which might fit the description of the Snowman, the orangutan is the most likely. But although his Malayan name means "man of the trees" (*orang*=man, *utan*=trees), we are inclined to doubt the similarity, since the orangutan is principally a tree-dwelling anthropoid of Borneo and Sumatra.

Nevertheless, there do exist two points of similarity between the orangutan and the descriptions we have of the Snowman. In the first place, they both commonly have tan-colored hair, and the orangutan is large enough to fit a certain species of Snowman. In the second place, and this is a most singular factor, the feet of the orangutan are shaped so that they bend at the ankle, possibly to facilitate his tree-climbing, and only the borders of his feet would normally touch the ground, leaving no marking of his instep.

Various travelers to the Himalayas have deduced, from the creature's tracks, that he is a bear, rather than an anthropoid. Some characteristics of the bear family (Ursidae) are the short tail and the claws which do not retract, characteristics which differentiate it from the feline family.

The bear may be found in most portions of the northern hemisphere, including Europe. He may also be encountered in the southern Malayan archipelago and in the Atlas Mountains of Morocco and Algeria. He also exists in the southern Andes. The bear found in the Himálayas is the *Ursus arctos isa ellinus*, and differs only slightly from the European species. Generally, it is slightly smaller and its coat is of a paler color.

The *Melursus ursinus* is found in diverse regions of India and in the foothills of the Himalayas, in places usually associated with the Snowman. This bear has a tail which distinguishes it from other species, a rough, dull coat, and a large tongue, which is quite useless for collecting honey from wild honeycombs. The paws of this bear are large and very powerful. It is much smaller than the black bear of the Himalayas. If we were to asssume that it is our enigmatic Snowman, we would have to assign it a much greater stature.

From the time when evidence (vestiges and tracks) began to surface for the existence of an "unknown" living being in the Himalayas, Mongolia, and even North America, there has been controversy. The vestiges, patches of hairy leather which have been found, are on view in some of the monasteries in the Himalayas. Numerous artifacts of this nature have turned out to be really the hides of deer.

Much more reliable evidence has been supplied by the photographs of Snowman tracks. These photographs were obtained by Eric Shipton on the Menlung glacier, during an expedition to explore Mount Everest in 1951. Eric

Shipton was in the company of Michael Ward and Sen Tensing. At 22,000 feet, tracks of 12 1/2 by 6 1/2 inches were found, as measured against an ax handle.

The clarity of the images—which show clearly the thick impression of the toes, the contours of the foot, the tracks which were left in a regular line over the snow—demonstrate that the tracks were not those of a leopard or a bear, nor those of a langur monkey. Unfortunately, further evidence of the Shipton expedition is rather vague.

According to Shipton, he followed the tracks until he lost them in the darkness. By morning, glacial winds had obscured the tracks, and Shipton never caught a glimpse of the creature. Shipton's story was confirmed by Sen Tensing, his Sherpa guide, who confided that two years before he had actually seen a yeti. The creature was covered with reddish hair, except for the face, and had a large, sharply pointed head, which was also covered with thick, reddish hair.

Despite sightings of the Snowman by Sherpa tribesmen, most anthropologists find their stories questionable and think that they are merely the expression of an ancient legend. According to this legend, a monkey king was converted to Buddhism. Although he went into the hills to live as a religious recluse, an ogress fell in love with him. The children she bore him had tails and were covered with hair, and these were the first yeti.

A later reference is in the sixth book of the Hindu classic the *Ramayana*, entitled "Sita Lost," written possibly as early as the third century B.C. The passages refer to some supernatural creatures, called Raksha (singular) and Rakshasa (plural). Rakshi-Bompo is the name of a type of Snowman found in Nepal. Other Himalayan names for this tree-dwelling demon are Kaughi, Bang, Banmanche, Ban Vanas, and Van Manas, as well as other names.

Another reference to the Snowman is cited in *Man* (August 1959), a monthly review of the Royal Anthropological Institute. The article, "Proofs from the Old Literature on the Existence of the Snowman in Tibet and Mongolia," was written by Emmanuel Vicek, of the Archaeological Institute of the Academy of Science of Czechoslovakia.

Abominable Snowman: Legend or Reality?

The author describes drawings of the Snowman which are to be found in a book kept in the library of the University of Gandan. The volume, which first appeared in Peking at the end of the eighteenth century, was reprinted a century later in Ulan Bator, capital of Outer Mongolia, which is close to where the sighting of the Snowman by Christopher Dodson and Dr. Rinchon occurred in the spring of 1959. That portion of the book which deals with the flora and fauna of Tibet is full of illustrations. The Snowman appears together with drawings of monkeys, leopards, eagles, and diverse beasts. All the animals are realistically drawn and easily recognized. There is nothing suggestive of a naturalized mythology.

Modern evidence for the existence of the Snowman began as the British occupation of India spread to the foothills of the Himalayas. In the nineteenth century Nikolai Prsvalsky, a Russian colonel, reported a fleeting glimpse of an Almas, a primitive animal-like creature, during his exploration of Mongolia and the Gobi desert. The suggestion that this creature might be related to man, however, caused Indian authorities to discourage, if not tacitly prohibit, further scientific investigation.

The first crack in this wall of silence came in 1913 when a group of Chinese hunters wounded and captured a manlike creature whom the Sherpas called a Snowman. It is said to have been kept at Patang, in Sinkiang province, for five months before it became ill and died. According to the descriptions of that time, it had a black, monkeylike face and was covered with silvery yellow hair several inches long. It had exceptionally powerful hands and its feet were shaped more like those of a human than an ape. It grunted and made guttural sounds, but spent most of its time pursing its lips and making whistling noises quite loudly.

The outbreak of World War I made further exploration difficult, but on April 27, 1915, Henry Elwes, Himalayan botanist and explorer and member of the Royal Zoological Society, read a letter before that august body. The letter was from one J.R.P. Gent, forester of the Darjeeling district, in which he mentions the possible existence in Sikkim of a huge monkey, unknown to science.

The beast, Gent declared, was of great stature and was only to be found in cold climates. It was covered with shaggy, grayish-yellow hair, and able to walk upright. His tracks were forty-five to sixty centimeters in length and fifteen centimeters in depth.

In 1921, William Knight, a member of the Club of the Royal Society, sent a communication to the *Times*, London, in which he recalled a conversation he had had with the editor of that newspaper some years before. At that time, he had occasion to note that he had told several members of his expedition of what he believed to be a sighting of the Snowman. The group had been following a river in the Gangtok region, and Knight had fallen somewhat behind as they passed through a thickly wooded area. While passing through a clearing, he saw the Snowman at a distance of fifteen or twenty feet. It was an unusually close sighting, a fact which gives added weight to Knight's description.

The creature was six to seven feet high and yellowish in color. There was little hair on his face. He stood upright, and his hands, arms, legs and chest were formidably large. He carried what appeared to be a primitive bow. He did not see Knight, who remained quite still. He was able to observe the creature for five or six minutes. He seemed to be watching some man or animal at the foot of the hill. When finally he moved, Knight was amazed at his rapidity.

That night, during dinner at the hotel in Gurkha, Knight mentioned what he had seen to the guests. In the morning, he mentioned the incident to one Claude White, but did not recall the details of their conversation. Unfortunately, he did not record his impressions at the time, nor did he even write his letter to the *Times* until he read of snow tracks discovered by an expedition to Mount Everest.

Colonel C.K. Howard-Bury, leader of the 1921 Mount Everest expedition, found snow tracks which seemed to be those of a human being. This occurred at Lkaka La, a pass on the northeast side of the mountain, at an altitude of about 19,800 feet. His bearers told him that they were the tracks of the "savage man of the snows." As a joke, Colonel Howard-Bury cabled his information to London, but the cable was taken seriously, causing a general sensation and the rise of new rumors about the Snowman.

In 1925, Nicholas Tombazi saw what was possibly a yeti in Sikkim. Two years earlier, British Major Alan Cameron and his party were working their way toward the peak when one of the guides spotted a line of living creatures moving slowly along a cliff face, well above the snow line. When they reached that cliff face two days later, they found giant, manlike tracks in the snow. After these sightings, there were no further significant ones until the Eric Shipton expedition in 1936.

Tracks were found around the snow line, and H.W. Tilman followed them for several miles, noting that they ran one behind the other, in a manner no four-footed creature uses. Tilman finally lost them in a long stretch of barren rock.

In 1937, a British explorer, Frank S. Smythe, in the company of two Sherpas, stumbled upon "impressions of a great foot, apparently that of a biped." Upon being questioned, the Sherpas replied, probably to please their patron, that they were the footprints of the Snowman, and much later, with the same indifference to fact, did not hesitate to sign a document stating their belief. Smythe photographed the footprints.

Smythe came out of Tibet with reports of a manlike, wild creature of an unknown type, which frequented the upper reaches of the Himalayas, living on grubs and rodents and larger animals when he could get them.

The photographs were sent for examination to various zoological institutions, which declared that the footprints could very well be those of a bear, even though there were discussions as to what species of bear.

Found at the 14,000-foot level, measurements of the prints showed they were remarkably human in shape, but the stride was such that one foot imprinted its toes in the heel mark of the other. The size was about thirteen inches long by five inches wide.

World War II again reduced the number of sightings, but one particularly vivid experience occurred to Slavomir Rawicz. A Polish official, Rawicz escaped from a Soviet prison camp in 1942. With his companions, he marched across Mongolia to the Himalayas. While resting, they observed a pair of bipeds at a distance of about 330 feet. Rawicz later described a type of beast which was intermediate: a mixture between a bear and an orangutang, seven to eight feet tall.

New controversies sprang up again in 1951, after the Everest expedition of Eric Shipton, when he returned bearing very clear photographs of the tracks of some mysterious being.

In an effort to clarify the mystery, the Natural History Section of the British Museum and the Zoological Society examined the Shipton material and drew two theoretical conclusions: the snow tracks either belonged to a bear or were made by the paws of a langur monkey, even though no langur had been known to leave tracks anything like the length of the ones in the Everest photographs.

H.W. Tilman, in an article entitled "Himalayan Monkeyshines," asked the question, "And what became of the monkey's tail?" There ought to have been marks of the tail in the snow, just as there would have been of the paws, since the tail of the langur is quite long and constitutes one of the most notable parts of its anatomy. Tilman, in a caustic manner, suggested that perhaps in order to live at those altitudes the langurs used their tails as a muffler.

Some of the new information which appears from time to time could be called "proofs," other of it simply "declarations." For example, there are occasional and alarming stories of encounters between the natives and beings with the aspect half-ape and half-man, usually taking place in the depths of the jungles or forests or on riverbanks. Most native evidence, however, may be disregarded because it is the narrative of frightened and unsophisticated people. But even at this level of accuracy, we cannot dismiss the evidence out of hand, but must distinguish between the declaration of an eyewitness and more concrete proof.

One of the most reliable witnesses to the existence of the Snowman has been Sir John Hunt, the leader of an Everest expedition in 1953. He mentioned in letters as early as 1937 that he had discovered two series of mysterious tracks on a hill beneath the Yemu glacier. On this later expedition, he and his companion, the Sherpa Pasang, followed a path of strange snow prints until they disappeared on the ice of a glacial crest. They appeared to have been descending the rough further side of the glacier.

Sir John believed at first that the tracks were made by the same creature whose tracks had been found by a German expedition, more or less in the same area. Pasang became nervous when he described those tracks. It was only later that Sir John discovered that the German expedition had not passed through Zemu La, nor had any other expedition in the course of that year. This story is typical in that it may induce us to doubt the Sherpa's story about any earlier tracks, but it does not explain the tracks which Sir John found.

Based upon Shipton's photographs and an accumulated number of sightings, proofs for the existence of the Snowman have become more abundant, reliable, and significant. Among more recent researchers, none has performed more valuable experiments than Vladimir Tschernezki. A zoologist who has worked in England, Tschernezki possessed a variety of moldings and drawings which helped to reconstruct the Snowman. Some of these are based on comparisons between the figure of a gorilla and that of the Snowman. His general impression of the Snowman was published for the first time in the Manchester *Guardian* in 1954.

It is Professor Tschernezki's view that if we reconstruct the footprints of some indeterminate being between monkey and man, our reconstruction will be similar to tracks photographed by Shipton. The footprints of the Snowman, nevertheless, show several peculiar characteristics, always assuming that what we are examining is the tracks of a specialized branch of higher anthropoid. The footprint of the Snowman is about 12½ inches, or somewhat less than that of the largest gorilla. The depth of the track is more than 2½ times that of the gorilla. Consequently, this anthropoid of the Himalayas ought to be larger and heavier than the largest of the simians of which we have any knowledge. Professor Tschernezki writes: "Also you will recall that the superfice of the sole of the foot of the monkey is much more narrow than that of man, especially toward the heel. The depth and massive structure of the heel of the Snowman is impressive. Its 'human' character is even more pronounced in the Snowman than in modern man and in the human fossil of the Neanderthal. From this evidence, we are able to deduce that this being possesses feet of an extraordinary thickness and mass, feet that are much stronger than that of any extant or extinguished simian, and that it is not similar to any human foot, either fossil man or present man. Its relative largeness and the position of the toes is also peculiar. The first toe is exceptionally thick. The third, fourth, and fifth are narrow and placed close to one another. The second toe is of an intermediate size, between the first and the third, and widely separated from them. This formation appears to indicate that this toe has the capacity for movement independent of the other toes. This ability for grasping, and the strength of the feet, would make it ideal for traversing rocky ground and climbing the highest slopes."

From the Shipton photos, it is possible to deduce that this being walks with his feet farther apart than does a man. The gait appears to have a deep lateral movement, with the body inclined forward.

Some months after the publication of his article, Tschernezki had completed the work which was to serve as the basis for the introduction to a scientific book which he was thinking of publishing. He had enlarged the photographed footprint to its actual size, and a plaster of Paris mold was designed according to the structure indicated by the footprints.

The Shipton photographs had retained certain special details, such as the impression of each toe and the small portions of snow in the separation of each digit. From this form, it was possible for Prof. Tschernezki to establish, in an experimental way, the usual posture of this mysterious being.

The track discovered by Shipton was modeled and enlarged to its natural size. With the artificial foot he had produced, he made tracks in the snow and then compared the results with the original. He also reproduced the artificial tracks of a mountain gorilla and compared them.

The results of his experiments showed:

(1) That the artificial track produced by the model was very similar to the original photo. This signifies that Tschernezki's model is also very similar to the foot of the Snowman.

(2) That the artificial foot of the mountain gorilla is very similar to the reconstructed foot of the Snowman, much more closely resembling it than any other living animal.

The structure of the model foot of the Snowman shows the following particularities:

(1) The foot is huge: its length, 12½ inches, is equal to the foot of one of the largest gorillas. Its width is truly enormous: 7½ inches, tapering down to 6½ inches at the heel. These measurements suggest a massive bone structure, similar to the Neanderthal whose remains were found in the Crimea.

(2) The depth of the heel of the Snowman appears to be abnormal, especially if we consider it as representing a primate (excluding man), which necessarily possesses a narrow and pointed heel.

(3) The *hallux*, or deep gorge of the foot, of the foot of the Snowman is larger and thicker than that of the gorilla. This larger deflection should help it to walk, grasp, and climb.

(4) The second toe is extraordinarily large and thin. This is a peculiarity of the foot of the Snowman. The tendency to lengthen of the second metacarpal bone is a very well-known sign in human fossils. The famous Russian anthropologist G.A. Bonch Osmolovski describes the foot of the man found in Kiik Kolba in these terms: "The great length of the foot of the man in Kiik Kolba is related to the lengthening of the carpo and all the metacarpal bones. The length of the foot in relation to the first and third digits is smaller than that of present-day man. In the fourth and fifth digits, on the other hand, they are much larger."

The abnormality of the heel and the second toe of the Snowman show a grotesque enlargement of an evolutionary tendency. The highly developed second digit ought to play an important part in the creature's ability to walk.

(5) The digits of the Snowman could be summed up in

the following fashion: the second digit is the longest, the third, fourth, and fifth are small in comparison, and the toe is the shortest and thickest.

Since the investigations of Shipman and Tschernezki, research into the existence of the Snowman has been largely confined to further sightings and expeditions, including a Russian commission led by Dr. A.G. Pronin in the Pamir region of Central Asia in 1958. That same year, an expedition of the Czechoslovak Academy of Science, in collaboration with the Scientific Commission of Mongolia, corroborated the earlier work of Dr. Emmanuel Vicek.

Some researchers are so convinced of the existence of the Snowman, and in areas as widely separated as British Columbia and Azerbaijan, that they have devoted a lifetime to the study, notably Prof. Boris Porshnev, a Russian historian, and Prof. J.R. Rinchon of Outer Mongolia. Today, the work is carried on by their disciples, most actively by Prof. Jeanne Kofman, who had studied with Porshnev. She engaged for several years in field work in the Caucasus Mountains, where she collected circumstantial evidence and eyewitness accounts. She and her team found hoards of food, seemingly stolen by the mysterious creature and hidden in the tall grass. Her team's investigations took place from 1970 onward.

A great variety of theories, some verifiable and others merely speculative, have appeared periodically since 1921. During the past fifteen years, especially, there has been a sporadic mushrooming of theories. Among the strangest has been the idea that the snow prints are caused by atmospheric conditions, sharp changes in which cold air is followed by layers of warm air, causing variables in the humidity which were converted to water. This water, in turn, causes furrows in the snow, producing hollows. This explanation was accepted by only a few glacier specialists. Most of them pointed out that the atmospheric conditions required were pure supposition, and even if these conditions did produce hollows, these would appear as if created by chance and not in the form of regular patterns such as would be left by a living being walking through the snow. Furthermore, such hollows would not have the form of footprints, such as were seen in the photographs obtained.

The Himalayan theory, based primarily upon reports of the Sherpas, divides the Snowman into three categories. The largest of these types appears to be a vegetarian, except when driven by hunger to flesh-eating. The medium-sized Snowman is thought to be an aggressive predator, while the third and smallest, the Rakshi-Bompo, raids crops and flees when sighted.

Theories, hypotheses, legends, and new references to the Snowman emerge constantly. These are often contradictory, or so embellished as to turn them into instant legends.

It is worth noting, however, that much information eludes clear zoological identification, while sightings fairly consistently occur in geographic zones with the same natural flora and fauna.

Instances of these inexplicable appearances occur thousands of miles apart. The pattern of the sightings suggests the form of an S, stretching from North America to the Caucasus, across the Bering Strait. The most marked curve of the S is found in the mountains of Pamir, Soviet Union; after that, the Himalayas, Sikkim, and Butan, followed by the Mongolian deserts and mountains. From there a theoretical line could be drawn through the heights of northeast Siberia to the Bering Strait, which in the Pleistocene or Great Ice Age united Siberia with Alaska. From this point, an imaginary line could be drawn down northeast Canada and the Rocosas Mountains, with an extension as far as British Columbia, where legends of the Sasquatch, or "hairy man," are found, and, farther down, to the place of the California sightings. (In the northwestern United States, the Snowman is known as Bigfoot.)

Descriptions of the Snowman, or its footprints, always refer to mountainous regions covered with forests or very dense vegetation, nearly inaccessible to human beings because of snowdrifts or heavy rains.

Although the coastal belt of Alaska is filled with tundras and marshes, it is also considerably mountainous. For the most part, the mountain ranges are at a moderate elevation, but some are quite notable, such as the Brooks Range and the Mountains of Alaska. These elevations are considered by geologists to be a continuation of the Rocky Mountains. Near the coast, the Brooks Range descends to form plateaus, where erosions, rainfall, and lakes exist similar to those of the Himalayas and Mongolia.

Although most of the evidence for the existence of the Abominable Snowman is circumstantial, it does "hang together" and makes a fairly plausible case. What is needed is the hard-core evidence which zoologists and archaeologists require for their work. Until such evidence is found, it should be remembered that laughing at native tales of terrible monsters has not always been wise. The history of the natural sciences demonstrates this fact for us over and over again. One startling example occurred in the latter half of the nineteenth century when an American explorer, Paul Du Charilliu, brought home the skin and skeleton of a giant gorilla to confound the skeptics.

Eskimos, during the same period, were widely thought to be legendary creatures. Man, it was well known, could not exist without a vegetable diet, and there simply was no vegetation in the Arctic. It was later found that Eskimos secure their vegetable requirements, as do predatory animals, by eating the bowels of herbivores.

So far, no one has brought in the hide and hair of the Himalayan Snowman, let along captured some, but there is no reason to suppose this may not one day happen. Not all reports of the Snowman have been based on eyewitness testimony of laymen. There has been a good deal of scientific speculation as well, although often based on indirect or inferential evidence. For example, in September 1959, Dr. L.S.B. Leakey, of the Coryndon Museum of Nairobi, announced to the world that he had discovered the "missing link" between the South African gorilla and man. It was Dr. Leakey who disinterred the first skull, in the Olduvia Gorge, Tanganyika. He designated the find "the nutcracker man" because of the unusually large teeth, but also gave the species the more scientific name of *zinjatropo.* (Zinj is the ancient name for East Africa.) He estimated the age of the skull at 600,000 years. It is fascinating to speculate on the possibility that one of these creatures, or one closely related, still survives somewhere, unknown to us, perhaps in the high mountains.

In conclusion, we should continue to follow the most recent paleontological discoveries which tend to corroborate the hypothesis of a close relationship between the Snowman and the gigantopiteco. In recent years, the teeth of this enormous primate fossil and two corresponding lower mandibles were discovered in a cave in southern China. The structure of these mandibles shows that, anatomically, the gigantopiteco occupies an approximately intermediate place between the gorilla and the fossil of the *Paranthropus crassidens* of South Africa. Continued exploration may supply the answer to man's past.

The documents and testimony regarding the Snowman deal with "the impossible," contradict orthodox science, are unexplained and unexplainable. But the very possibility of the existence of such a creature shows us that man's world is still full of powerful, compelling mysteries, despite all the progress he has made. As Thomas Edison once wrote about the frustrating failure of some of his experiments: "They taught us a lot we hadn't known before and they also taught us how little we understand some of the things we do know."

The Mystery of the Crystal Skull

Paul Langdon

Few discoveries are totally unique, but the mysterious Crystal Skull which was unearthed in Honduras has no equal anywhere. Neither the craftsman who created it, the civilization of which it was a part, nor its symbolic or ritual meaning have become known. Mr. Langdon, who has written widely on esoteric subjects, regards the Crystal Skull as "one of the ultimate mysteries of any known civilization."

In 1924, a tall, grim-lipped explorer and his native bearers chopped their way wearily through the twisted green vines of British Honduras, opening a way into a matted clearing. Overhead, a vulture circled slowly and brilliantly plumed parrots screeched at these intruders into a land where no man had been for centuries. A jaguar growled nearby in the bush. A slimy poisonous lizard scurried across their path.

The white man was an archaeologist and modern soldier of fortune. He had endured the heat and the dangers of one of the world's thickest jungles because he was seeking clues to a civilization which had disappeared over four centuries before. He and his party of short, brown-skinned natives had hacked away at the heavy undergrowth for endless days, looking for ruins of an ancient city which the villagers had told him about. After months of searching, they stumbled upon the city—tinted greenish yellow by the sunlight filtering through the trees, resembling little more than a few huge mounds, it was so overgrown with foliage. They set to work quickly and eventually found what appeared to be a crude staircase, its stone steps leading up hundreds of feet to a flat crest. "There is what you seek, señor," whispered one of the bearers. "There is Lubaantún—'The City of Fallen Stones.'"

With Mitchell-Hedges, there were Lady Richmond Brown and Dr. Thomas Gann, a crotchety ex-medical officer, and, most important, Mitchell-Hedges' fifteen-year old adopted daughter, Anna. It was she who, three years later, while trying to remove a wall which had fallen on a ruined altar, first saw the crystal skull glittering in the dust. The skull had been buried beneath the temple altar, and three months later the matching jawbone was discovered twenty-five feet away. Lubaantún had given up the skull but kept its secrets to itself.

The man who since then has made the most thorough examination of the skull is Frank Dorland. Although he postulates that the radar-scanning of an installation near his home might account for some of the effects the skull produces, it cannot account for all of them. A colorless aura shines from the skull. The skull itself is without any tint, but the aura grows "strong with a faint trace of the color of hay, similar to a ring around the moon." And the phenomena are not limited to visual ones. At times sounds occur around the house. "It is much like an *a capella* choir," Dorland explains. "No instrumental music, but human voices singing some strange chants in a very soft manner. Then there are the bells. The sounds of bells, sharp and metallic, and quite high. No deep gongs or church bells, these are faint, quite high silver bells, very quiet but very noticeable. I have no explanation for these things."

Other odd effects are apparently associated with the skull's presence. Dorland goes on to say, "The skull exhibits and transmits to the human brain all the five senses: taste, touch, smell, sight, and hearing. The skull changes visibly in color and transparency, it exhibits its own unmistakable odor when it cares to, it plants thoughts in viewers' minds, it makes people thirsty, it impresses audible sounds on the ears of the viewers; those in meditation before the skull feel all this and they also feel physical pressures on their faces and bodies. When a sensitive person places his hands near the skull, distinct feelings of vibrations and energy are felt and the senses of both heat and cold depending on where the hands are held."

In addition to the rhythmic tinkling of bells and soft human voices, poltergeist effects seem to have been produced around the house. There have been unexplained bumps in the night and various other sounds. As far as other visual effects are concerned, Dorland has noticed, both alone and in the presence of others, that "the skull seems to be constantly in a state of flux, exhibiting changes of mood, clarity, and color. The front part of the skull has been observed to turn cloudy like soft cotton candy. The very center of the skull sometimes turns so clear it seems to disappear into a vast void. The skull itself in total has changed in color from clear crystal to shades of green, violet, purple, amber, red, blue, etc. The visual study of the skull has strong tendencies to exert hypnotic effects on the majority of viewers."

This last point is particularly important, since crystal is such a highly refractive substance. It is as easy to read images into it as it is to see human and other shapes in clouds. Patterns diffuse and dissolve with the slightest change in illumination or in the viewing angle, so that the skull makes an excellent speculum for crystallomancy. That such effects may also be the effect of intense concentration or meditation cannot be ruled out. Nor, for those who are easily suggestible, can the hypnotic effects the skull produces—especially when it is illuminated—be ruled out as a possible explanation.

Claims that the crystal skull has caused or even can cause death should most likely be filed right next to the curse of old King Tut. But what did F.A. Mitchell-Hedges himself believe with regard to these occult stories? Our only answer comes from his daughter, Anna. In the March 1962 issue of *Fate* she wrote: "My father believed that the skull brought death only to those who did not revere it, who laughed and jeered at it. He lived for thirty years after he first found and took possession of the skull. During that time he survived eight bullet wounds and three knife attacks. He did not pray to the skull, but he treated it with the same reverence that he believed the priests of the Mayan civilization had for the skull. After all, to them it was almost akin to a god."

In a letter she wrote to Richard Garvin on January 30, 1970, Anna said, "I will not have the skull used as a crystal ball." For this reason she asked that the skull be returned to her possession. It was her intention to bequeath the skull to an American Indian museum, where it would be safe from the prying eyes of sensation hunters.

What is there about the skull which might have given rise to such sensationalism? To begin with, the skull is an exquisitely crafted, highly realistic piece of sculpture, its crystal encapsulated with veins and bubbles when it was formed. The mineral itself possesses a natural purity and is unscratched, indicating that its delicate intricacies were shaped without the use of metal tools. For example, the zygomatic arches (the arch of the bone that extends along the front or side of the skull) are oddly relieved and separated from the skull itself. These arches employ principles strangely similar to our modern optics. They channel light from the base of the skull into the excavated eyesockets. There miniature concave lenses focus the beams to the rear of the sockets themselves.

These hand-ground and natural prisms and lenses channel light from the base and distribute images and shapes. A set of concave and convex lenses gathers light rays focused at the base of the skull and transmits them directly into the eyesockets. Such is the "power" of the skull that we may well imagine that the ancient Mayans employed it in some religious ritual. For example, if the skull were suspended over a small hole on the top of a hollow altar, and a fire lit beneath it, most of the light would be reflected into the eyes of the skull, causing them to flicker eerily and hypnotically, and the entire skull would seem ablaze.

Further, the snugly fitting jawbone can be moved up and down. And as author Richard Garvin has noted in his

The Crystal Skull, "The skull itself balances at a point where two tiny bearing holes are drilled on each side of its base and bottom. It seems to have been skillfully designed to receive counterweights. If the skull were placed on a hollow altar with all its mechanisms working, this would be the picture: its eyes would flicker and glow wildly; the jaw would open and close; the head would nod approval or disapproval with the barest breath of air—a macabre, animated sibyl."

Finally, as Dorland discovered, there is an interior ribbon prism which can be observed by looking into the upper surface. Objects can thus be magnified and viewed when held beneath the skull. These images of light could be projected from the rear of the eyesockets.

For all the artistic virtuosity and painstaking technical care which went into the making of the skull, it remains merely a magician's prop. Dorland wonders why so much energy should have been expended, unless it was the product of a declining civilization, used by priests to keep the masses under control. The laws of whatever strange society inhabited Lubaantún, therefore, would seem to have been made by the priests, who would have most probably used the crystal oracle to also control the king and his military.

However, the Mayan civilization appears to have been centered upon the role of the priest from earliest times, although the death cult appears to have been introduced by the Toltecs in the late ninth century, at a time when the Mayan culture had commenced its mysterious decline. The Mayas first appeared on the historical scene about 200 A.D., scattering throughout the eastern jungles of southern Mexico, Guatemala, Honduras and British Honduras, and eastern portions of San Salvador. The Mayas came to power in 400 A.D. and were the most brilliant and advanced civilization in the New World until about 850 A.D. They remained a vital force in Central America until the arrival of the Spanish in the early 1500s.

The Mayan civilization first began to emerge under the influence of the Olmecs, their neighbors to the north (near present-day Vera Cruz). About a thousand years earlier, the Olmecs had begun building stone monuments and had developed a form of writing. The earliest Mayas were probably small groups of farmers who cultivated maize, pepper, manioc, pumpkins, vanilla, cocoa, and cochineal. For meat, they hunted wild pig, jaguars, and alligators. They traded primarily in rubber. For domestic animals, they had dogs, pigs, and turkeys. Their structures and carvings were almost certainly of wood.

About 400 A.D. they began to make stone images of their gods, and finely carved stelae recorded dates in a complex astronomical calendar. Sacred monuments were placed in the courtyards surrounding the pyramids, on the top of which fine temples were built and decorated in the most brilliant mineral colors. Most of the "cities" so far discovered have not, in fact, been cities at all, but religious centers which served the people on the surrounding farms and villages.

C.A. Burland, author of *The Ancient Maya*, writes: "Their level of civilization was high, since they had great artists, mathematicians, and astronomers. Carvings show us that they could produce beautiful woven cloth, and dressed magnificently in garments and headdresses which showed many grades of social rank. They invented a kind of paper on which they painted books inscribed in a syllabic script which included some 650 symbols. Yet this magnificent civilization was without the use of metals. Gold was sometimes imported in small quantities from Panama; copper and bronze remained unknown. Maya culture was supported by a simple Neolithic type of agriculture brought up to the limits of efficiency."

The Mayan civilization suffered other odd limitations. There is no evidence that they had discovered the use of the wheel nor that they possessed work animals. They performed odd mutilations on themselves, such as strapping boards to their babies' heads so that their foreheads would develop a sharp backward slant. Small children had balls suspended between their eyes so they developed permanent cross-eyed squints. Adults pierced their noses and lips and inserted gold-and-jewel plugs.

Something went wrong with this first phase of high culture about 850. Suddenly and catastrophically, for some reason archaeologists are still trying to discover, the Mayas began a mass migration out of Guatemala, Honduras, and southern Mexico. One by one, the great cities such as Tikal and Palenque, were abandoned, sometimes so rapidly that buildings still under construction were left unfinished. Some of the Mayas migrated south, but most of them moved north to the Yucatán peninsula, where they immediately began to build entirely new city-temples, including the famous Chichén Itzá and Uxmal.

With regard to the "lost cities" of the Mayas, the question is not *where* they went, but *why* they went.

Some scholars suggest there may have been a terrible civil war; others have suggested that earthquakes (similar to the one which shook Guatemala in 1976) may have driven the people from their settlements. However, there is no trace of physical damage at the sites. Others think that a climatic change led to the rapid spread of the jungle; others claim it was disease, possibly yellow fever or malaria, that felled the earlier Mayan culture. However, the Mayas remained numerous and vigorous enough to rebuild their culture, and they moved only a few hundred miles away, so it appears disease and climatic changes may be ruled out. One imaginative theory suggests that a prophecy was followed and that the people left their homes at some predetermined date. There is a historically recorded instance of such a migration after the Spanish arrived. Mayan civilization had become locked in time. Their priests had become so concerned with timekeeping and calendar-making that they predicted the end of the world and ordered everyone to leave. But when the world kept on spinning, why did they not return; why did they begin again? And what part might the sibylline crystal skull have played in the migration?

Most probably, however, the Mayas simply ate their way out of house and home. They practiced an agricultural procedure known as "slash-and-burn," a technique still used in many parts of South America and Africa. By this method, the farmer clears the land by chopping down the brush, burning the weeds and vines, and then planting the seeds below the ashes. The next season the old crop is burned off and new seeds sown. Within a number of years, the earth becomes exhausted.

The burned land must be allowed to lie fallow for several seasons, growing over with weeds and vines until its natural nutrients are restored. As their populations grew, Mayans would have required more and more food to feed the priests, government administrators, soldiers, and court retainers, and the farmers would have been forced to cultivate land farther and farther from the center. The distance between field and market would then have grown so great that the farmers could not easily have brought in their harvest. Angered by forced labor, with its implicit taxation (since the priests and other aristocracy consumed food but did not work), the farmers simply wandered off into the jungle. Eventually the priests and rulers would have realized that the land could not support them, and they moved themselves and their people north to found new cities in more fertile lands.

Unfortunately, the Yucatán Mayas would never regain the levels of science, art, and culture which they had known in the highlands. Their small villages did survive in the almost waterless limestone peninsula of Yucatán when underground streams were turned into fully exploited waterways. No longer was the high priest of a city ranked equally with *Halach Uinic* ("ruler of men"), who had been previously educated in religious magic. In the Yucatec cities, the palace of the civil ruler was in a position of equal importance to the temple of the gods. Each city was an independent state, often at war with its neighbors. They preserved the old calendar in part, but were unable or unwilling to use the ancient counts covering vast distances in time.

As these Mayan cities were being erected, they were invaded by the Toltecs, a warlike tribe from north of Mexico City. As sometimes happens with invasions, the conquering but more primitive Toltecs were absorbed into the culture of the defeated Mayas, with one notable exception. The influx of Toltec thought did force the Mayans to adopt the Toltec belief in the god Queztalcoatl, "The Plumed Serpent," and in human sacrifice.

With the help of Mayan artists, the Toltec nobles settled down to build an even more glorious city than their old one at Tula, which had been destroyed in a disastrous war.

Although this city of Chichén Itzá was very Mexican in style, they quite soon abandoned their simpler picture writing for the more useful Mayan script. Apart from their architecture the later Mayas were not very successful as artists; they were better historians, however, than their ancestors, as would befit a people with a much shorter time sense. Each city had its Book of Chilam Balam (Book of the Jaguar Priest). Here, very short and usually inaccurate accounts were given of the major events of each twenty years, and events were projected into the future. They still believed that all events were tied to a rhythm of fate and must happen again whenever the calendrical elements were the same.

About 1200, the various Toltec chieftains warred constantly among themselves, and Chichén Itzá was destroyed about 1200–1250. A new center was founded at Mayapan, but it never achieved an important place in Mayan culture. When the Spanish arrived three hundred years later, the Mayas were divided and disorganized, and fell easy victims to the conquistadores.

Although the Mayas must have viewed the fall of the Aztecs with some trepidation, it was not until 1526 that the de Montejos, father and son, made two successful assaults on the Yucatec Mayas, but in 1537 they surrendered. Many of the Mayas once again migrated and founded the city of Peten Itzá on the shores of Lake Tayasal. Here they remained undisturbed until 1702, when the Spanish destroyed this last remnant of Mayan culture.

Was the crystal skull the product of the highland Mayas? Did it play a role in their abandoning their cities? Or was it fashioned by the Toltec-infused Yucatec Mayas? It will be remembered that at Chichén Itzá virgins were decked with gold, jade, images of rubber and bone carvings, and thrown into a "well" sacred to the rain gods as sacrifices. Enormous ball courts, with tiers of stone seats, were built between temples, and there the game of *pok-o-pok* was played for mortal stakes. The earliest form of the game was played by the Hohokam Indians of Arizona and was carried into Central America by the Toltecs, a Plains Indian of northern Mexico, where the Mayas transformed its rules into a sacred ritual.

A large sculpture on the eastern wall of the ball court at Chichén Itzá shows seven players gathered around a ball decorated with a human skull. Two spiral carvings that arise from the jaw of the skull spell out the Mayan word for death. One of the players holds a flint knife in his right hand and the severed head of an opposing team member in his left. The decapitated body lies at his feet, and seven serpents come from its neck, perhaps symbolizing the death of the entire seven-man losing team. Some experts think the sacred ball game may have stood for the eternal cycle of life and death, with the ball representing the sun in its path across the sky and the result somehow predicting the fate of the harvests and the fortunes of the city the following year. This ball game, too, was a form of human sacrifice, and one which the spectators no doubt enjoyed. What role might the crystal skull have played in these ancient rituals? Remembering that modern scientists have judged that the fashioning of the skull with sand and other primitive means would have taken three hundred years for its completion, should we date it pre- or post-Toltec in its origin?

Before attempting to speculate on an answer, let us look at the history of the skull itself and the life of the man who discovered it. F.A. Mitchell-Hedges was a man only partially interested in pre-Columbian history; he was primarily concerned to find evidence for the existence of the lost continent of Atlantis. The son of a financeer, Mike, as he was called, yearned to be free of a structured society. While a student at University School, London, he poured over the novels of H. Rider Haggard and Robert Louis Stevenson, and the lost lands and prehistoric animals of Arthur Conan Doyle. But in particular he was drawn to the pre-Columbian civilizations.

Ironically, his first chance for adventure came from a friend of his father, Brooke Mee, who jokingly offered him a chance to join an expedition into the Norwegian Arctic. Reluctantly his father agreed, hoping he would be cured of his wanderlust. He returned hoping to become an explorer, but he was seventeen, and soon found himself working for his father's stockbroker. By February 1900, he had saved a few hundred pounds and left for Canada, hoping to find gold in the Klondike.

In Montreal he happened upon a man named Clarence McCuaig who convinced him that to really make money he would have to go to New York. McCuaig was influential in financial circles, and his letter introduced Mike directly to J.P. Morgan. Between playing poker and buying the right stocks, he accumulated ten thousand dollars (no small sum in those days) and made plans for going to Central America, but his mother fell ill and he had to return to England.

In England, he met and married his first wife, Lillian ("Dolly"), and set himself to making money. As the years went by and there were no children, he made and lost several fortunes, until the day came when he secured Dolly in a cottage and set out once again for Central America, without a cent. It was November 1913 and he was thirty-one years old.

For months he bummed around the Southern states, mostly in Louisiana and Texas, trying to raise enough money to get across the border by playing poker and working as a ranch hand. Finally, he won five hundred dollars at a gambling casino, got into his ancient car, and headed for Mexico. He had not been in Mexico a week when he was mistaken for an American and captured by Pancho Villa's men. Upon convincing them he was an Englishman, he was allowed to choose whether he wanted to ride with them. He elected to do so, but this adventure was soon to end. Pershing had invaded Mexico with twelve thousand troops, and England was now at war with Germany. Mike pleaded with Villa to let him return to England, and to his surprise Villa agreed.

In London, he was rejected because of a leg wound he had suffered with Villa, and so busied himself with volunteer work until the summer of 1917, when he found himself in Ontario, Canada. After a night of drinking too much rye with two Americans, Mike found himself the unwilling parent of a ten-year-old orphan girl named Anna-Marie Le Guillon. Not wanting to leave the girl in his room alone, the two maudlin drunks had simply desposited the girl in his room. Angry and surprised, but having always wanted children, Mike decided to make the best of it. He rejected the thought of putting her in an orphanage, so there was simply no other choice for him.

And that was the way he met the person who, a decade later, would actually discover the crystal skull.

By the end of the War, Mike had once again restored his fortune in New York. He was thirty-seven when he once again set out for Mexico, this time with a twelve-year-old girl in tow. But the journey proved too difficult and he sent her to stay with a friend in New York. Mike continued to search, driven by his belief that a portion of Atlantis had once been off the coast of Honduras and that the Bay Islands were a remaining fragment of the lost continent. He even experimented with underwater exploration, but without equipment, he was doomed to failure. Finally, in 1921, he returned to England to raise money for a full-fledged expedition.

He was repeatedly turned down, of course. But luck seems never to have left Mitchell-Hedges for very long. He chanced to meet a woman, one Lady Richmond Brown ("Mabs"), whose doctors had told her that she had only a short time to live. With a life that offered her nothing but the prospect of an exciting adventure, she willingly financed him.

As matters turned out, Mabs did not die, but lived to accompany Mike on many expeditions. Those of the Bay Islands lasted several years and provided the basis of the British Museum's present collection of Chunaque Indian fetishes. In 1924, their attention was turned to the mainland, partly by Mike's conviction that there was a lost city which would aid his Atlantean researches, and partly because a special meeting of the legislature of British Honduras was held, which passed an act granting them exclusive rights to excavations for the next twenty years.

In the years that followed the 1927 discovery of the crystal skull, Mitchell-Hedges and his party continued to find priceless objects, both on the islands and the mainland, upon which much of our present-day knowledge of the pre-Columbian world is based. The authenticity of his finds received wide endorsement. George C. Heye, director of the Heye Foundation of the Museum of the American Indian in New York, wrote in 1935: "Your own observations, and the United States Government surveys in Nicaragua, prove conclusively that at some remote period a tremendous earth movement of cataclysmic force must have taken place in that part of the world . . . and that your excavations have actually unearthed the cultural artifacts of a prehistoric people that existed prior to the great earth movement. . . . your discoveries open up an entirely new vista in regard to the ancient civilizations of the American continent."

Not all archaeologists, however, have been so kind to Mitchell-Hedges. His free-swinging life-style, his belief in Atlantis, which sometimes led him to wildly misdate his findings, his lack of any formal training in archaeology— all have made him suspect to many of his colleagues. Nevertheless, he opened Central America to archaeological exploration, and while his evaluations may be suspect, his findings are not. When he died on June 12, 1949, aged seventy-seven, Mitchell-Hedges might have looked back on a full life, upon a position secure in the history of archaeology—but he did not find Atlantis.

Nevertheless, it is still reasonable to ask, was Mitchell-Hedges right after all? What does the skull itself tell us? To begin with, it is made of crystal, and the very word "crystal" comes from the Greek *crystallos,* or "clear ice." (The name "quartz" was first used by Georgius Agricola in 1530 and is an old German word of uncertain origin.) Substances such as crystal, diamonds, glass, rock salt—all fascinated ancient man; they were like frozen holy water from heaven. Heaven was supposed to be a vast sea of glass from which the all-vital "rain" was sometimes distilled, but in a way over which man had no control. The shifting, cloudy imperfections of crystal were images of departed souls. As early as 4000 B.C., the Egyptians placed a crystal "third eye" on the forehead of the dead before mummification, so that they might be able to see their way in eternity.

However, the symbol of the skull did not exist to any extent in Egyptian times. The skull as a symbol of death is a product of Hellenistic and medieval times, and is largely confined to Christianity. On the other hand, skull worship is found in primitive cultures throughout the world. The skull is worshiped and saved, for it was believed to be a magic talisman of the godhead, of all-encompassing knowledge and wisdom. From this belief arose the practice of headhunting and, in a later, modified version, of scalping.

In both pre-Hispanic and modern Central America, the skull motif occupies a central place. For example, the center of the Aztec calendar is a skull; Quetzalcoatl's twin brother Xototl was represented by a skull; the skull was an important thematic element in the mosaic inlays of the Nahuas and the goldwork of the Mixtecs. It is in common use today in Mexico, not only on ceramics, arches, and various craft works, but in the tiny candy skulls which are so popular with the children, and especially on the Feast of All Saints—or Halloween.

Mineralogical and morphological examinations of the crystal skull by scientists tell us that the piece was carved from a single clear block. The skull itself measures five inches high by seven inches long and is five inches wide. It weighs eleven pounds, seven ounces, and it is valued at more than $250,000. While it is not hard to find larger and heavier pieces, they inevitably are tinted, usually green, amber, or a dirty tan. The crystal of this skull is quite clear.

As we have noted, the skull was examined by Hewlett-Packard, the world's largest manufacturer of electronic test equipment, computers, and oscillators used in time and frequency standards. Most of the firm's quartz is mined in Brazil and arrives variously colored and no more than fist-sized. The results of the examination indicate that the original crafting was probably done with a combination of sand and water—and patience. The polishing was probably accomplished by a compound of silicon sand and tiny fragments of crystal applied in a poultice. However, quartz crystal is scarcely less hard than diamond and extremely hard to work with. No dating of the skull seems possible, beyond the three hundred years Hewlett-Packard estimates that it took to fashion the piece.

Frank Dorland has suggested that possibly the skull was of European origin and that it was fashioned on the commission of a king and arrived in the New World sometime late in the 1700s. Such an explanation is possible, of course. It is even possible that Mitchell-Hedges acquired the skull in Europe and planted it in Lubaantún for Anna to find. Dorland also contends that many of Mitchell-Hedges' expeditions were secretly financed by William Randolph Hearst, an avid collector of *objets d'art* for his castle at San Simeon.

Unfortunately, there are two difficulties to this idea. First, although Hearst certainly knew of the skull, because he often ran stories about it in his newspaper, the old New York *American*, he never acquired the skull. Except for a brief period, 1928–29, when "Mike" loaned it out to acquire money for his next expedition, it never left his possession, or even his bedside, until he bequeathed it to Anna. Secondly, if it is of European origin, we must then suppose that it was made upon the order of a king, or rather a dynasty, who then employed a succession of artists for three hundred years, and none of this is known in our history. The thought is absurd on the very surface, and made further absurd by the fact that no secular artifact of man has ever been fashioned over a three-hundred-year period. Mankind will simply not work that hard on an *objet d'art*, nor will he sustain the interest for generations. But man has worked that hard and harder when he was inspired by religious motivation. Christianity has never provided such a motivation for crystal skulls, but the religions of the Americas did.

In March 1971, Dr. Frederick Dockstader, one of the world's leading authorities on pre-Columbian art and head of the Heye Foundation of the Museum of the American Indian, expressed this opinion in an interview with Frank Dorland: "During the time from 1575 to 1650, the art of rock-crystal carving flourished in Europe. And during that period a great many Old World objects were traded back and forth at that time. Any object such as the skull would have much greater value than objects made from materials native to the area. But the most intriguing thing is that the jawbone is separated. This is most unusual and not found in skulls either in Europe or the Americas. I'm inclined to believe that it was used during the Aztec period. The possibility of the skull being Mixtec in origin seems the most probable but that probability itself is quite remote."

George Kennedy, of the Institute of Geophysics and Planetary Physics at the University of California at Los Angeles, does not agree with Dr. Dockstader, but neither does he think it came from British Honduras. "I have great doubts if the skull ever came from Lubaantún," he wrote in a letter of February 1971, to Dorland. "Stylistically it is reminiscent of a great number of late Aztec objects which were normally carved by Mixtec artisans in the employ of the Aztecs. The style suggests that if it were authentic pre-Columbian, it would have to date from somewhere between 1350 and 1500. To the best of my knowledge, Lubaantún was a site abandoned around the year 800. Thus, on style grounds it's hard to believe that a late Mixtec carving would be found in a Maya site abandoned 600-700 [years] earlier."

Clearly, both experts' opinions abound with contradictions and simple vagueness. Dockstader allows that it might be either European or American in origin, and then discounts that opinion because of the detachable jaw. He then suggests the "quite remote" but "most probable" opinion that it is of Mixtec origin. Kennedy then suggests that the "style" is reminiscent of the Mixtec, but that if it is authentic, it could not have been found in Lubaantún. The implication is clearly that Mitchell-Hedges, or someone, had found a Mixtec sculpture and planted it at Lubaantún, then allowed it to be found by someone else. This is rather a strong suggestion, but certainly it cannot be ruled out of the question. The difficulty is that neither Dr. Dockstader nor Mr. Kennedy appear to account for the three hundred years it would have taken to create the skull. Perhaps there is a simpler hypothesis.

Let us begin with the fact that no crystal skull of nearly anything like the size and purity of this skull is known. The Aztec or Mixtec skull in the British Museum, found in Mexico in 1889, is substantially smaller and, more important, of far inferior workmanship. Let us also begin with the difficulty that quartz crystal of the size and purity required for this skull was not available in Central America. Such unsculptured crystal was, however, to be found in northwestern Mexico, the location from which the warrior Plains Indians moved.

It is possible that Mayan trade routes reached that far north in the pre-Toltec era, but it is highly unlikely. A more probable hypothesis is that the Toltecs brought the unsculptured block of crystal with them when they overran the Yucatec Mayas about 875. Even as the later Aztecs were culturally inferior as artisans to the Mixtecs, so the Toltecs were to the Mayas. By their victories, however, they were able to enforce their religion and utilize the higher but subordinate culture. Then, assuming the fashioning of this particular skull was begun about 900, it would have been completed by 1200. With the internecine wars that followed and with the fall of Chichén Itzá in about 1225, it is quite probable that the Mayas may have taken the skull with them to Mayapan, and more probable that they began to reoccupy old sites after the arrival of the Spaniards, including Lubaantún.

This hypothesis has at least the virtue of accounting for all the known facts and of not contradicting any of them. On the other hand, there is no substantive proof for this theory. The mystery of the crystal skull remains, one of the many mysteries which surround and enrich our lives, and perhaps, after all, Mitchell-Hedges was right: the skull is a fragment of the lost continent of Atlantis. If so, it is a time bomb waiting to explode amid conventional science. And perhaps we are better off, after all, if we never solve the mystery of the crystal skull, for it arouses in us a sense of awe and wonder, and so long as the mystery remains a mystery, we are left with a crystal eye into eternity.

ABOUT THE EDITOR

Martin Ebon is an authority on a wide variety of topics in the fields of social and political science. His articles and reviews have been published in periodicals ranging from *Human Behavior, The Psychiatric Quarterly,* and *Contemporary Psychology* to magazines such as *The Saturday Review, The Humanist,* and *The Naval Institute Proceedings.* Mr. Ebon served for many years as Administrative Secretary of the Parapsychology Foundation and subsequently as a consultant to the Foundation for Research on the Nature of Man.

Martin Ebon has authored numerous books for New American Library. Among the most recent are THE CLONING OF MAN: Brave New Hope—or Horror?, THE SIGNET HANDBOOK OF PARAPSYCHOLOGY, PROPHECY IN OUR TIME, DEMON CHILDREN, and THE WORLD'S WEIRDEST CULTS. Mr. Ebon divides his time between his homes in New York and Athens, Greece.

SIGNET Books You'll Enjoy

SIGNET Books of Special Interest

☐ **DEMON CHILDREN edited by Martin Ebon.** Terrifying but true case histories of children suddenly transformed by demonic forces into creatures of evil, documented by leading psychic investigators. Stories range from the original incident on which *The Exorcist* was based to the tragedy of a young child enslaved by a Tahitian god. (#E7986—$1.75)

☐ **FORTUNE IN YOUR HAND by Elizabeth Daniels Squire.** An expert hand-analyst and syndicated columnist provides a step-by-step illustrated do-it-yourself guide to enable readers to gain insights into character and personality through interpretation of signs in the hand. (#E8061—$1.75)

☐ **ADVENTURES INTO THE PSYCHIC by Jess Stearn.** A fully documented account of every major aspect of the occult field today, it takes the reader through a series of psychic experiences, ranging from ESP, seances, and telepathic crime detection. (#J9376—$1.95)

☐ **THE SUPERNATURAL by Douglas Hill and Pat Williams.** Two knowledgeable authorities, both of them journalists, lead an excursion into the realms of the unknown, presenting astonishing facts about witches and vampires, ghosts and poltergeists, grotesque cults and orgiastic rituals. (#J9265—$1.95)

☐ **ALIENS FROM SPACE . . . THE REAL STORY OF UNIDENTIFIED FLYING OBJECTS by Major Donald E. Keyhoe (USMC Ret.).** From secret Washington archives, eyewitness testimonies and official scientific findings, new astounding evidence about Von Daniken's ancient astronauts and their landings on Earth today! (#J8968—$1.95)*

☐ **WE ARE NOT ALONE by Walter Sullivan.** Winner of the 1965 International Nonfiction Prize, this is a comprehensive account of the search for intelligent life on other worlds, by the Science Editor of *The New York Times.* (#J8168—$1.95)

* Price slightly higher in Canada

Buy them at your local

bookstore or use coupon

on next page for ordering.

Related Titles from SIGNET

☐ **MANY MANSIONS by Gina Cerminara.** The most convincing proof of reincarnation and ESP ever gathered in one volume. A trained psychologist's examination of the files and case histories of Edgar Cayce, the greatest psychic of our time.
(#E9290—$2.25)

☐ **THE COMPLETE BOOK OF MAGIC AND WITCHCRAFT by Kathryn Paulsen.** A thorough depiction of specific rites, recipes for potions, a glossary of terms, and a vivid history of magic make this work invaluable reading for anyone interested in magic and the occult. (#E9180—$1.75)

☐ **ADVENTURES INTO THE PSYCHIC by Jess Stearn.** A fully documented account of every major aspect of the occult field today, it takes the reader through a series of psychic experiences, including ESP, seances, and telepathic crime detection. (#W7822—$1.50)

☐ **KATHRYN KUHLMAN: The Woman Who Believes in Miracles by Allen Spraggett.** In this inspiring story of the greatest faith healer since Biblical times, Allen Spraggett gives a number of indisputable case histories of the cures that Kathryn Kuhlman has effected. (#W8529—$1.50)

☐ **THE TAROT REVEALED: A Modern Guide to Reading the Tarot Cards by Eden Gray.** A fascinating and authoritative introduction to the ancient art of the Tarot cards. Special Feature: A special order blank is in the book so that you can order a Rider-Waite Tarot Deck. (#E9510—$2.25)
